BUDDHA

TAO

ZEN

Mystic Triad

To sit alone with a book
from unseen generations
is a pleasure beyond compare.
-- Yoshuda Kenko
(1283-1350 CE)

PREFACE

Why another book on the wisdom of Asia? As one who has attempted for 55 years to translate the *Book of Tao, I Ching, Tibetan Book of* the *Dead,* and *Analects* of "Confucius," never from originals (we have none) but always from copies of copies, it became apparent it is difficult to know the original meaning. Over many centuries of time there was an opportunity for the most dedicated scholars to "put a spin" on what was translated. Add to this the fact that the earliest teachings were not written but recited and passed on by word-of-mouth 500 years before being set down in writing, then when written passed from one language to another and across differing subcultures.

It is not an easy task trying to recapture original meaning. Yet, despite all the problems there is the glimmer of truth consistent across time, language, and culture. To see it, leave behind all preconceptions, sometimes prior knowledge, and be "as wide open as the sky."

The compiler of this material is a retired clinical psychologist who spent 30 years treating thousands of people with problems. It made him a good listener and hopefully an impartial judge of mental processes. Those skills helped him grasp the meaning, manifest and latent, in ancient teachings. A part of him that emerged over decades of reflecting on Asian wisdom is *roshi no-name*. *Roshi* means one who reflects teachings, never his own, and *no-name* (note lower case!) reminds him of the danger of indulging one's ego or selfish self.

Roshi and the psychologist met 55 years ago over the *Book of Tao.* It was West meeting East and surprising to both, they got along well. The psychologist "saw" current psychological concepts in the ancient teachings. *Roshi no-name* "saw" ancient teachings in current psychological concepts. This continues to fascinate both of them.

So, that's why there is another book on the wisdom of Asia. It is the first written by a psychologist trained and experienced in seeing into and through words for ultimate meaning. Every available translation was used after decades of reflection. *Roshi no-name* says there is more meaning *beyond words than in them*, that words read hurriedly, superficially, are like a quick hello but with unhurried reflection are more like a warm hug. May it be so for you!

THE TARGET...

1. Buddha's "message from the heart," his Four Noble truths and 8-fold Path.

2. The cosmic consciousness of Tao, the transcendent and transcending force that enriched Buddhism for 1000 years.

3. Zen mind, the "direct pointing" insight of Dhyana Buddhism from its India roots to Ch'an in China and Zen in Japan.

   ... synergized in a Mystic Triad.

NOW, THE ARROW...

1
BUDDHA HEART

This I have heard.
Accept or reject it.
Either way, go in peace.
-- Buddhist greeting

HINDU ROOTS

Buddha was born and raised Hindu, so Hinduism was a major influence in his life and thought. A brief history of Hinduism helps to better understand Buddhism. Hindu civilization was highly developed in the Indus Valley 2000 BCE or earlier. Indo-Aryans settled in the Punjab with a predominantly male pantheon of gods and warrior ethic. By 900 BCE Indo-Aryans moved to the Ganges Valley. From its beginning in the 5th century BCE, Buddhism interacted with Hinduism.

Hinduism flourished in the Gupta Empire (240-550 CE) when many temples were built. Rituals were preserved in the *Puranas*. Many Hindu sects evolved. There are six classic Hindu philosophies:

1. **Nyaya**, the logic of Akshapada Gautama (6th century BCE).
2. **Vaisheshika** based on the atomist reality in nine substances: earth, water, light, air, ether, time, space, soul-self, mind, and their qualities, activities, and inherent truth, of Kanada (3rd century BCE).
3. **Samkhya,** combining two basic principles of soul (*purusha)* and materiality (*prakriti)* in the three *guna* of light and goodness (*sattva*), activity and passion (*raja*), and dark inertia (*tama)* of Kapila (6th century BCE).
4. **Yoga** in the *Yogasutra,* by Patanjali (2nd century BCE).

5. **Purva/Karma Mimamsa,** the *Vedas,* interpreted in ritual and rules, from Jaimini (2nd century BCE).

6. **Vedanta** "end of Vedas," non-dualist monism, reality as illusion, from Shankara (788-820 CE), *Advaita Vedanta,* and *Ishishta Advaita* of Ramanjua (ca 1017–1137 CE).

SCRIPTURE. The Vedas are the Hindu scriptural authority. The oldest of four is the *Rig-Veda,* 1028 hymns to gods (*Samma Veda*), sacrifices (*Yajur Veda*), and magic spells (*Atharva Veda,* added about 900 BCE), *Brahman* myths and rituals (about 600 BCE), and the *Upanishads* (mystic meditations). *Vedas, Brahmas,* and *Upanishads* are *shruti* ("from the gods") and cannot be changed. *Smrti* ("what is remembered") can be revised and include the epics *Mahabarata* and *Ramayana* and "textbooks on sacred law" (ca 300 BCE-300 CE). Translations vary. The *Purana* were composed later and are other myths, hymns, rituals, and philosophies on creation, deities, human genealogy, and also references to the Sun, *Shiva/Vishnu* and *GaneshaSkanda.*

COSMOLOGY. The universe is perceived as a great sphere or cosmic egg, with concentric circles of continents, oceans, heavens and hells. India is in the center. Time cycles from a golden age (*Krita Yuga*) through two deteriorating periods into *Kali Yuga,* the present age that will end when the universe is destroyed by fire and flood. A new golden age will follow. Human life also cycles. At death the soul leaves the body to be reborn in another life or non-life form, according to the law of *karma.* Bad karma can be redeemed by renouncing worldly ways and attaining final liberation or *moksha.* Non-violence (*ahimsa*) is an aspect of *moksha.* Vegetarianism is part of *ahimsa* that forbids blood sacrifices. The *Bhagavad Gita* describes three *moksha* paths: (1) good deeds, ritual, and sacrifice (*karma path*); (2) knowing the Upanishads and meditation (*jhana path*); and

(3) devotion by songs, poems, and the Upanishads and epics (*bhakti path*).

GODS. There are many gods but all are aspects of the one great *Brahma*. *Indra* is king of the gods, of fertility and storms. *Agni* is the god of fire. *Shiva* has many forms (human, animal, and vegetable) and is the deity of the *Kapalikas* who carry skulls to remember *Shiva* beheading his father, *Brahma* who must carry his skull until he attains *moksha*, *Pashupatas* who worship *Shiva* as Lord of beasts, and *Aghori* "to whom nothing is horrible" and who eat meat. According to legend, a lotus sprang from *Vishnu's* navel from which *Brahma* was born. *Vishnu* created the universe, heaven and earth, and rescues them. He is incarnated as humans *Rama* and *Krishna*, animals, fish, the dwarf trickster *Vamana*, man-lion *Narasimha*, and *Rama-with-axe Parashurama* who killed his promiscuous mother. There are many minor gods such as monkey god *Hanuman*, *Rama's* assistant *Skanda*, son of *Shiva*, general of the army of the gods, and *Ganesha*, the elephant-head god, remover of obstacles and the god of scribes and merchants.

GODDESSES are aspects of *Devi*, the Divine Mother. *Shakti Female Power is* worshipped in ritualized forbidden sex and consuming forbidden substances of meat, fish, and wine. *Devi's* peaceful aspects are in wives of gods, such as *Brahma's* wife *Sarasvati, Lakshmi the meek* (*Vishnu's* wife), *Parvati daughter of the Himalayas*, and *Ganga, goddess of the river, music, and literature.* As *Durga the Unapproachable* she killed the buffalo demon *Mahisha*. As *Kali the Black* she dances on corpses, then eats them. She also rides a white horse to destroy the universe at the end of each Kali age and appears in animal and fish forms.

RITUALS. Many Hindu ceremonies are rites of passage (*samskaras*) such as birth, surviving the first week, first time a child eats solid food, boy's first haircut, girl's first menstruation, marriage, pregnancy, delivery, funeral, and annual offerings to ancestors. Women are believed to have the power to intercede with gods and a daily ritual of a Hindu wife is to offer fruit or flowers (*puja*) to gods, good or evil spirits, local spirits, even to snakes, at a shrine in the house, garden, crossroads, or other special places. There are thousands of local temples, many no more than a cloth effigy with a basin for hand washing, and large temples, temple cities, and caves, some with ornate carved stone. On special days a god's image is taken from its shrine and carried around the temple complex on a finely carved wood chariot.

CASTE. According to the *Svadhamma* everyone is born for a specific task and begets children to do the same. The primary goal is a son to make offerings to ancestors. Another goal is to unify the soul (*Atman*) with the Universal Soul (*Brahman),* and liberation (*moksha*) from rebirth. The highest three castes are the priestly Brahman, warrior *Kshatriya,* and *Vaishya* general public.

JAINISM (Jain Dharma)

Jainism is an ancient religion in India dating back to Lord Mahavira (540-468 BCE), the 24ᵗʰ Tirthankava ("river crosser") and *Jina* ("victor over the samsara"). He was human (Jainists have no gods). When he was 30 he became a radical hermit, depriving himself and meditating for 12 years. He then taught for 30 years that the universe is alive, everything in it sacred, and thoughts, words, and actions attract karma that clings to the soul. At age 72 he chose to fast to death "to burn out bad karma."

Jainism is based on five vows called *mahavratas*: do not kill, steal, lie, own anything, or have sex. By following vows *moksha* libration is realized. No gods or spiritual beings can help. *Ahimsa* non-violence is a basic value. Jains respect all life forms and are strict vegetarians. They value spiritual independence. The three jewels of Jainism are right belief, knowledge, and good conduct. Speakers from other religions are welcomed. Jains run hospitals for humans and animals. It is estimated there are more than three million Jainist monks, nuns, and lay people in India.

BUDDHA'S MESSAGE FROM THE HEART

Buddha, in Sanskrit means "awakened or enlightened" and there have been many Buddhas. Acceding to one legend, Siddhartha Gautama became the 4th Buddha, called "the compassionate one." Maitreya is the 5th Buddha and is awaiting birth. Siddhartha taught a system of character development to realize enlightenment (*nirvana*), liberation from rebirths. Unlike Hinduism's seemingly endless chain of rebirths, he taught that nirvana can be achieved within one's own lifetime. He used meditation more than rituals and his "message from the heart" is more psychological than religious. In fact, his teachings are consistent with current psychological concepts. Buddhism is as much a psychology for personal growth a practical system of therapy as a philosophy or religion. Alfred North Whitehead described Christianity as "a religion seeking metaphysics and Buddhism is metaphysics that generated a religion."

According to legend, Siddhartha Gautama, later to become a Buddha, was born in the 5th century BCE in a forest in Lumbini, Kapilavastu, near Nepal. His mother died a week later. His family was Hindu, of the Sakya or Shakya clan, a priestly-warrior caste. His father was Suddhodana, the tribal leader and Siddhartha was expected to succeed him. A holy man prophesied he would be a great leader but if he saw pain and suffering his compassion would cause him to leave home and be a great spiritual leader. Suddhodhana tried to prevent his son from seeing any pain and suffering by keeping him at home surrounded by positive surroundings.

When Siddhartha was 18 he married Yasodhara, probably an arranged marriage. One day he persuaded a servant to take him to the village and despite his father's order that streets be cleared of anyone sick or suffering, Siddhartha saw **the four sights**: a frail old man, a sick man, a dead body in a funeral procession, and a holy man in rags begging for food but smiling, seemingly content. The pain and suffering troubled him greatly but he was also fascinated with the poor hermit's serenity.

When he was 29 he left his wife, pregnant with son Rahula, to search for the meaning of life and how to end suffering, called **The Great Renunciation.** It is said he realized that if he waited for the birth of his son he would never want to leave. For six years he lived as a hermit near Gaya, Magadha, meditating and fasting with five others. One day, as he bathed in the Phalgu River he was so weak he had to hold on to a hanging tree branch to return to shore. He fell and would have died but Sujata, a herdsman's daughter, gave him some rice-milk. He then realized the hermit life did not help him find the meaning of life or how to relieve suffering, nor did his previous rich life. He returned to a normal, modest diet.

When he was 35 he sat seven days facing east under a fig tree in Gaya, Bihar. Under a full moon he attained **nirvana,** called **the Great Enlightenment**. The tree is now called **the tree of wisdom,** the **Bodhi** or **Bo tree.** The five ascetics with him became followers. His first public teaching was in the Deer Park at Sarnath where he explained **the Four Noble Truths and Noble 8-fold Path.** It is said 900 were converted. 60 were sent "to spread the Dharma." Buddha's teachings are called the **first turning of the Dharma wheel.** He required followers to greet others with: "This is what I have heard. Accept or reject it.

Either way, peace be with you." Buddha taught 45 years and was 80 when he died, surrounded by 600 monks and nuns.

Buddha taught by word-of-mouth, **the oral Dharma.** The earliest writings appeared about 150 BCE and became the **Theravada tradition, the teaching of the elders,** also called **Hinayana** (lesser vehicle) because it is based on the **Arhat** "lone rider" model of individual enlightenment. It spread when Emperor Asoka (ca 273-232 BCE) was converted and sent out missionaries. **Mahayana Buddhism, the greater vehicle** (a carriage for many, not an Arhat lone rider), the **2nd turning of the Dharma wheel,** emerged about 100 BCE but its seed ideas were evident immediately after Buddha's death. **Vajrayana Buddhism, the 3rd turning of the Dharma wheel,** came to Tibet from India in the 8th century CE by Padmasambhava. There are many sects but all accept the **Four Noble Truths** and **8-fold Path.**

1st NOBLE TRUTH (*dukkha*, wheel)

Existence means pain. Every living thing knows pain, is born in pain, dies in pain and thus, some life pain is inevitable. The symbol of the First Noble truth is the wheel of destiny or fate.

2nd NOBLE TRUTH (*tanha*, wheel's hub)

Craving is pain, the wheel's hub. Most of life's pain is from selfish craving. Buddha called it "a fire that can consume." We want what we don't have and are not satisfied with what we do have. We tend to be more selfish than selfless and hold on to things rather than share them with others. We want more, not less.

3rd NOBLE TRUTH (*nirodha, hope*)

The message of the Third Noble Truth is: It need not be so! You have within you the way to overcome suffering and karmic destiny (rebirths) and realize enlightenment (*nirvana*). It is a message of hope, that the flame of craving can be extinguished: "Lamps flicker when their oil is spent" (Edwin Arnold, *The Light of Asia*).

4th NOBLE TRUTH (*magga, deliverance*)

There is a way out: the **Noble 8-fold Path,** eight steps of self-mastery that Buddha called "a wide path open to all" and "forging these eight links do not bind but free. They free you from yourself and from themselves."

THE NOBLE 8-FOLD PATH

These eight steps do not have to be taken in order. They interact and overlap. Most translations refer to each step as "right" but this can be taken to mean there is only one way and anything else is not right. It may be more useful to think of each step as a *better* way and in this book each step is referred to not only as *right* but also as a *better* way.

1. RIGHT (BETTER) VIEW
(*Samma Ditthi*)

What is *really* true? This is the "wake up call" of the 4th Noble Truth, a better view, attitude, and orientation. Some interpret it as the right or true doctrine (*dharma* or *dhamma*). Buddha said failure to realize and follow this step causes more suffering than any of the other steps. It requires right understanding and a right view or attitude toward self, others, truth, evil, suffering and its cause, impermanence and change, and being open to ultimate truth and reality, aware of the **ten demerits** of killing, stealing, envy, lying, gossiping, malice, harsh language, vanity, sexual misconduct, and wrong views from ignorance and delusion.

Realizing this step is seeing a purely individual self as unreal illusion. This empowers you to see clearly what is there, not what you want or expect to see, have been taught to see, or are afraid to see, what is important and what is trivial, good and not good for you, and how thoughts and feelings, words and actions help or hinder personal growth and spiritual development. It is "seeing without naming" or labeling because that rigidly identifies, fixes, and judges.

ChuangTse (c. 300 BCE), a Tao master called "the second sage" after LaoTse and the *Book of Tao,* wrote: "There is nothing greater than a pine needle. Compared to it, even a mountain is less impressive." And: "The serenity of the wise is not what the world calls serenity. It comes from within and nothing can disrupt it. It is like still water, a mirror and model of serenity. If still water gets its serenity from being still, how much more the mind? So, the mind of the wise serenely mirrors the universe and everything in it."

SIMILAR WESTERN IDEAS

When I was 14, my father was so ignorant I could hardly stand it. When I was 21 I was astonished at how much he learned in seven years (*Mark Twain).*

Nature is the expression of a definite order with which nothing interferes, and the chief business of mankind is to learn that order (*Thomas Huxley).*

I do not know what I appear to the world but to myself I seem to have been only a boy on the seashore, now and then finding a smoother pebble or prettier shell while the great ocean of truth lay all undiscovered before me (*Isaac Newton).*

All nature is but art unknown to you; all chance, direction you can't see; all discord, harmony not understood; all partial evil, universal good; and, despite pride and erring reason, one truth is clear: Whatever *is* is right (*Alexander Pope*).

A little bit of learning is a dangerous thing. Drink deep or taste not the Pierian spring. Shallow draughts intoxicate the brain, and drinking deeply sobers us again (*Alexander Pope*).

2. RIGHT (BETTER) INTENT
(*Samma Sankappa*)

This step has also been interpreted as determination or purpose, with "a mind clear of clouds and fog" committed to good and doing good, not harming anyone or anything, and cultivating loving kindness and caring for others. This requires seeing you are not who or what you may think you are, or what others see in you, and resolving to be the best you can be, doing the best you can wherever you are, whatever you're doing. Buddha said: "Allow unkindness to die a natural death and make your life gentle as a soft breeze. Let everyone and everything be without judging, and relate to them with loving kindness." It is like taking a mental shower cleansing yourself of bias, freeing you of prior conditioning and preconceived notions, insulating you from anger, hate, and wrongful behavior. Buddha also said:

All we are is the result of what we have thought. It is founded on our thoughts and made up of our thoughts. Speak or act with an evil thought and suffering follows like the wheel follows the hoof of the ox that pulls the cart. Speak or act with a good thought or action and happiness follows like the shadow that never leaves you. Hate does not cease by hate. Hate ceases only by love. This is an eternal law (*Dhammapadda, Chapter 15*)

From MengTse (Mencius):

We should not live by experience alone but by what transcends experience, assured as much by what we do not see and have never seen as what seems real, and a duty to realize a sphere above and beyond what is only human conduct.

LiehTse or LiehTzu (c. 450 BCE) wrote *The Classic of Perfect Emptiness,* though some scholars suspect he was a pen name for ChuangTse because style and content are similar. An excerpt:

There is form and what makes form, sound and what makes sound, color and what makes color, taste and what makes taste. Form originates in matter but what makes it is not material form. Sound is heard but what makes it is unheard. Color is seen but what makes it is unseen. Taste is experienced but what makes it is in the tongue. All this is the principle of inaction. To truly re-alize bright or dull, caring or uncaring, sweet or bitter, brief or lengthy, treble or bass, specific or vague, present or absent, is to be unknowing yet all-knowing, powerless yet all-powerful.

SIMILAR WESTERN IDEAS

Many people think they are thinking when they are only rearranging their prejudices (*William James*).

The meeting of two personalities is like the contact of two chemicals. If there is any reaction both are transformed (*Carl Jung*).

A foolish consistency is the hobgoblin of little minds, adored by little statesmen, philosophers, and diviners. With consistency a great soul has simply nothing to do (*Ralph Waldo Emerson*).

There is nothing either good or bad but thinking makes it so (*Shakespeare, Hamlet*).

3. RIGHT (BETTER) INTERACTION
(*Samma Vaca*)

Better communication is to speak truth simply, kindly, or in silence. Buddha said we should use words "as arrows that strike without pain or in a silence that blesses everyone."   Realizing this step is to speak heart to heart, to join and not separate, heal and not hurt, simplify and not complicate or confuse. The goal is harmony in word and deed, saying the right word at the right time in the right way. If you know nothing or have nothing to say, then say nothing. Do not lie or use malicious, impolite, or harsh language or speak idly or foolishly. Speak heart to heart, to join and not to separate, to heal and not hurt, simplify and not complicate or confuse. The goal is harmony in word and deed, saying the right word at the right time in the right way.

Buddha said that "wrong speech hurts and cannot heal." He warned against five kinds of wrong speech: lies, slander, harsh words, glib talk, and idle chatter. He described five kinds of right speech as truthful, reliable, sincere, modest, and consistent. His advice when verbally attacked: "As the elephant endures the arrow so you should patiently bear with abuse. There are many unkind archers in the world." And in *The Thousands* (*Sutta Pitaka*, Chapter 8) Buddha said:

Though a speech is 1000 words but all senseless,
one word is better which when heard brings peace;

Though a poem is 1000 words but all senseless,
one word is better which when heard brings peace;

Though 1000 poems are recited but all senseless,
one word is better which when heard brings peace;

Though you conquer 1000 times 1000 warriors,
it is a greater victory to conquer yourself.

SIMILAR WESTERN IDEAS

What's in a name? That which we call a rose by any other name would smell as sweet (Shakespeare, *Romeo and Juliet*).

My reverence is for a holy simplicity, not wordy vulgarity (*St. Jerome*).

Some books are to be tasted, others to be swallowed, and some few to be chewed and digested (*Francis Bacon*).

4. RIGHT (BETTER) CONDUCT
(*Samma Kammanta*)

Buddha said: "Let every action weaken a fault. As weeds are removed before seed is sown, remove unwanted weeds from the garden of your mind. There is nothing with such power to prevent evil as right effort." Realizing this step is to avoid extremes and excess and focus on doing good, honestly, sincerely, and with loving kindness. And, if you can do no good, do nothing. It is accepting graciously and humbly only what is freely given, not taking what is not yours, and being content with what you have, not indulging in excess. It is to accept whatever befalls you, living each day as if it were your last because some day it will be. It is sharing in the happiness of others. Buddha said: "Let your love show in good deeds like gold threads in fine cloth. As you see your reflection in a mirror, so you should reflect on what you are doing." He warned: "There is no fire like lust. Passion does not die out, it burns out." And in the *Sutta Pitaka* Buddha observed:

Plant a thought and reap an act;
Plant an act and reap a habit;
Plant a habit and reap a character;
Plant a character and reap a destiny.

Also in the *Sutta Pitaka* Buddha said:

As wind blows down a tree, temptation overthrows those who live only for pleasure, are immoderate, lazy, and weak. As wind cannot blow down a mountain, temptation cannot overthrow those who live without pursuing pleasure, and are moderate, diligent, and strong. Rain leaks through a poorly thatched roof and craving leaks into an untrained mind but cannot leak through a well thatched roof. Craving cannot leak into a well trained mind. Those who recite the teaching but do not practice it are like those counting the cattle of others. They are not true followers of the Way. Those who can repeat little of the teaching but live it, do not crave or hate, are not deluded, and cling to nothing in this or any other world are true followers of the Way.

From MengTse (Mencius, c. 300 BCE):

What is a good person? We call someone we like a good person. Someone who is good we call a real person. We call one who is full of good a beautiful person. We call someone great whose good brightly shines. We call someone a sage who whose goodness transforms others. We call someone a sage whose goodness is beyond our understanding.

SIMILAR WESTERN IDEAS

The quality of mercy is not strained. It drops as the gentle rain from heaven upon the plane beneath. It is twice blessed. It blesses who gives and who receives (Shakespeare, *Merchant of Venice*).

If I speak the languages of people and of angels but do not have love I am only like a sounding gong or clanging cymbal. If I have the gift of prophecy, understand all mysteries, have unlimited knowledge, and faith that can move mountains but do not have love, I am nothing. If I give everything to the poor and even give up my life but do not have love, I gain nothing. Love does not delight in evil. It rejoices in the truth. It always protects, trusts, hopes, and perseveres, and it never fails (*I Corinthians* 13:1, edited).

5. RIGHT (BETTER) LIVELIHOOD
(*Samma Ajiva*)

Work should awaken, activate, satisfy, fulfill, and purify the mind. Choose work you can love, love it, and work because of that love, not for the work itself. You should work because you love, not because you love work. Realizing this step I value life as a mission, not a career, that living is giving, and the great law of life is love. You get to keep only what you share or freely give. Buddha called it "pure livelihood" that values life and men, women, and children as members of one family, and birds and animals as sharing life with us. It excludes livelihood that involves dealing in lethal weapons, poisons, intoxicants, animals for slaughter, or what could hurt anyone or anything.

6. RIGHT (BETTER) EFFORT
(*Samma Vayama*)

Energy (*virya*) appropriately used is needed to realize this step. The same energy can be vented in excess ambition or aggression or to grow spiritually and do good in a "declaration of strenuousness, a great victory" (*Angutarra Nikaya*) by the **four** great efforts of avoiding, overcoming, developing, and maintaining. Evil should be avoided and overcome if it is unavoidable. Have good will for all (*dana*) and help those in need (*sila*). It is to be humble and patient (*kshanti*), diligent in separating truth from error (*virya*), and to seek one-pointed concentration (*dharana*) toward selfless wisdom (*prajna*). The **five hindrances** should be avoided: sensual desire, ill will, doubt, lethargy, and needless anxiety. The key is not to fight them but become indifferent to them, the goal of the 7th step of the Noble 8-fold path.

SIMILAR WESTERN IDEAS

The spirit of God descended like a dove (*Matthew* 3:16).

I tell you the truth, anyone who has faith in me will do what I have been doing and even greater things than these (*Jesus, according* to *John* 14:12).

7. RIGHT (BETTER) MINDFULNESS
(*Samma Sati*)

Buddha explained mindfulness as "being heedful among the heedless, awake among those asleep, like a fast horse that overtaking slower ones." He saw an ego-self as a set of mental images and behaviors that interfere with awareness. Other words that help describe this step: attentiveness, wakefulness, heedfulness, and higher awareness. It is being keenly aware of what is and is not happening. The mind observes openly without comparing or judging as if for the first time, aware of sensed feelings, first impressions, and perceptions real or imagined.

Being mindful renders "I" to "it" then "I" fades "like a fog lifted by the sun." Sensing, feeling and thinking are noted as they arise as if by a friendly observer increasing the ability to rise above the sharp edges of experiencing. Needs are met with little or no anxiety. This is beyond Step 1 understanding because there is no discriminating, no comparing or evaluating. Buddha taught that mindfulness has four foundations: loving kindness (*metta*), compassion (*karuna*), altruistic joy (*mudita*), and equanimity (*upekka*).

Buddha recommended meditation (*bhavana*, "cultivating by looking into and through") to help develop mindfulness and He suggested the body, feelings, phenomena, and states of mind as objects of meditation. Others used: on Buddha, the Dharma, morality, and serene detachment. There are two major kinds of meditation, defined by their goals, *vipassana bhavana* "special sensing and perceiving," and s*amatha bhavana*. Both are further developed in Step 8.

Vipassana meditation prepares you to see, hear, and feel what's happening and how it changes moment to moment, without controlling or judging. Everyday living can then be experienced more as illusion and most behavior as superficial. It is mirrored thought *before* the mind names and interprets. There is some emotion when first experiencing it because of prior conditioning but it fades in time. As the need top control mental processes and distractions weaken, the mind is more serene. Any interpretation is only to choose what is more appropriate. It is a pure, neutral state of mind that exposes and neutralizes distorted thinking (craving, clinging, and delusion).

Samatha bhavana) seeks a serene mind by focusing on developing specific desirable traits such as loving kindness, sympathetic joy, compassion, and equanimity.

Regardless of the goal, breathing exercises are usually a starting point. **Mantras**, chanted or visualized words, parses, or symbols are used by many Buddhist sects. **Mandalas**, visual imagery in tapestries and sand trays, are used in Tibetan Buddhism (Vajrayana).

WRITINGS

FROM THE DIAMOND SUTRA

All living beings of any kind, born from moisture, eggs, wombs, or transformed, with or without form, thinking or unthinking, can and should achieve nirvana. Countless beings have thus been liberated, but none have been thus liberated. How can this be? It is because no real Bodhisattva sees any value in the ego as entirely separate, a personality free of all hindrances, or being as entirely independent (3).

Relying on material things is a delusion (5).

The highest truth is without limits and cannot be expressed in words. It neither *is*, because without it there is no reality, nor is *not*, because whatever *is* has limits to what it isn't (7).

You could fill countless worlds with treasure and give it all away, but if you take only these four lines and say and apply them, share, explain, and cherish them for the good of all it will be much more valuable:

> This is a fleeting world,
> a star at sunrise, a bubble in a stream,
> a flash of lightning in a summer cloud,
> a flickering light, a fantasy, a dream (22).

CHUANG-TSE (ca 300 BCE)

Suppose molten metal in the smelting pot said: "Make me into a sword." That metal would be discarded as unnatural. And if you said: "Make me into a man or woman" that, too, would be unnatural. We should be who we are naturally, as if awoke unconscious of the past from a dreamless sleep.

LIEH-TSE (ChuangTse?)

There is a creative principle itself uncreated and there is an unchanging principle that is in itself unchanging. One causes creation, the other causes change. What is produced continues to produce. What is evolved continues to evolve. This is an eternal law.

SIMILAR WESTERN IDEAS

People demand certainties, that this is true and that is false. There are no certainties (*H.L. Mencken*).

Between the idea and the reality, between the motion and the act, falls the shadow *(T. S. Eliot)*.

If you gaze long into an abyss, it gazes also into you (*Friedrich Nietzsche*).

Two prisoners look out the same window. One sees mud. The other sees the stars (*Frederick Langbridge*).

There is only one religion though there are hundreds of versions of it (*George Bernard Shaw*).

Truth is more important than the facts (*Frank Lloyd Wright*).

We are such stuff as dreams are made of and our little life is rounded with a sleep (*Shakespeare, The Tempest*).

There are more things in heaven and earth than are dreamt of in your philosophy (*Shakespeare, Hamlet*)

What a piece of work is man! How noble in reason! How infinite in faculty! In form, in moving how express and admirable! In action how like an angel! In apprehension how like a god! (*Shakespeare, Hamlet*).

The earth laughs in flowers (*Ralph Waldo Emerson*).

To ridicule philosophy is to philosophize (*Blaise Pascal*).

To live content with small means; to seek elegance rather than luxury, refinement rather than fashion; to be worthy not just respectable, wealthy but not rich; to study hard, to think quietly, talk gently, act frankly; to listen to stars and birds, to babes and sages, with open heart; to bear all cheerfully, do all bravely, await occasions, never hurry. In a word, to let the spiritual, unbidden and unconscious grow up through the common. This is my symphony (*William Henry Channing*).

8. RIGHT (BETTER) CONCENTRATION
(*Samma Samadhi*)

One-pointed concentration is the goal of this step. Buddha described it as a strong rope of the three intertwined strands of Steps 6, 7, and 8 that exceeds each of them. *Samadhi* means discipline or control. Meditation, an altered state of consciousness of calm reflection and serene detachment, is a way to realize this step. Buddhist meditation develops mental processes and differs from yoga that seeks to "yoke" to a cosmic consciousness. Buddha's goal was a calm reflective state of mind "beyond bliss and suffering, when the mind is pure and radiant as at birth. The unwise are half-filled vessels but the wise are like deep, calm lakes."

There are two meditation methods: *vipassana* and *samatha*. Traditional position is sitting upright on a pillow, legs crossed (full lotus not essential), first focusing on breathing, then an object, or mental imagery, usually once daily for 15-20 minutes. "White sound" or soft music helps. Some find incense helps. Four ways to meditate described in the *Sho-do-ka* of *Yoka Daishu*: (1) on still mind and body, the ideal; (2) body still but mind moving, as in reading or listening; (3) mind still, body moves as in walking; and (4) mind and body move, as in daily life.

Vipassana meditation prepares you to see, hear, and feel what's happening and how it changes moment to moment, without controlling or judging. Everyday living can then be experienced more as illusion and most behavior as superficial. The *Sho-do-ka* of *Yoka Daishu* suggests four ways: (1) on still mind and body, the ideal; (2) body still but mind moving, as in reading or listening; (3) mind still, body moves as in walking; and (4) mind and body move, as in daily life. Vipassana is mirrored thought *before* the mind names and interprets. There is some emotion when first experiencing it because of prior conditioning but it fades in time. As the need top control mental processes and distractions weaken, the mind is more serene. Any interpretation is only to choose what is more appropriate. It is a pure, neutral state of mind that exposes and neutralizes distorted thinking (craving, clinging, and delusion).

Samatha meditation seeks a serene mind by focusing on developing specific desirable traits such as loving kindness, sympathetic joy, compasssion, and equanimity. Both vipassana and samatha begin with breathing exercises.

Jhana are ancient pre-Buddhist meditation methods taught before writing and it is said Buddha used them before his enlightenment. Jhana means "state of meditative absorption" in Pali. There are eight of them and with practice they can be entered at will. They begin with access concentration and require some conscious effort and a less noisy ego-self. Jhana practice has been called "sharpening Manjushri's sword that cuts through ignorance and delusion." Manjushri is the Tibetan Bodhisattva of wisdom, depicted with a sword in his right hand and the sutra of truth in his left.

There are differences of opinion about Jhanas. They are called "a corruption of insight" in the *Visuddhimagga* and "dry insight" in the Burmese Mahasi Sayadaw Theravada tradition. The *Kevatta Sutra* considers them ways to paranormal powers (*siddhi*) more than for insight development. Some sutras show signs of addition, omission, or revision, making it difficult to know the original meaning. Some consider Jhana un-Buddhist by *wanting* to attain them (craving).

There are several ways to enhance meditation. **Mantras** are chanted or visualized words, parses, or symbols are used by many Buddhist sects. **Mandalas**, visual imagery in tapestries and sand trays, are used in Tibetan Buddhism (Vajrayana). **Mudra** are hand gestures that reflect a state of mind in meditation or teaching. Examples: **Namaskara** of greeting, reverence, or prayer, palms together; **Vitarka** of teaching and dialog, thumb and index finger forming a circle; **Dharmachakra**, representing Buddha's first teaching of the *Noble Truths* and *8-fold Path*, both hands in *Vitarka*, right hand outward, left inward, both over the heart; **Abhaya** of peace, protection, dispelling fear, right hand at shoulder height, arm bent palm out, fingers upright, left hand forward, down at side; **Bhumisparsha** earth-touching mudra of stability, right hand palm down on right knee, fingers down, left hand on the lap palm up in *Yin* openness.

BUDDHA'S LAST WORDS

Buddha died when he was 80 from tainted food and knew he was dying. It is said hundreds of monks and nuns were with him and his dying words were listened carefully, faithfully repeated, and later set down in writing:

Be an island unto yourself, a refuge to yourself.
See truth as an island and a refuge. Do not seek a
refuge anywhere else. Who, now and after I am gone,
is an island and a refuge to one's self, takes no other
refuge but seeks truth as an island and a refuge, will
reach the farther shore, but they must make the effort
themselves.

My age is now full ripe. My life is coming to an end.
I leave you. I depart relying on myself alone. Be earnest,
holy, full of careful thought, steadfast in resolve. Watch
over your own heart. Who wearies not but holds fast
to truth will cross the sea of life and bring an end to
suffering.

Do not weep. Do not be distressed. I have told you it is in the nature of things to eventually be parted from all that is near and dear. Everything born and develops has in it the means of its own demise. There is no other way than that a living being should pass away.

It may be some will say: "The word of the Teacher is no more and now we are without a leader." This is not so. The Dharma and rules I have given you will be your teacher after I am gone.

This I tell you: decay is inherent in all things. Work out your own salvation with diligence.

TEACHINGS

THE 12 NIRDANA

It is said Buddha first explained **the 12 nirdana** before he presented the **Four Noble Truths** and **8-fold Path**. The **nirdana** describe Buddha's developing insight that led to the **Noble Truths** and **8-fold Path**:

1. From ignorance (*avidya*) thinking divides unity into many forms (*samsara*).
2. From forms, consciousness emerges (*vijnana*).
3. From consciousness, mind-body awareness emerges (*namarupa*).
4. From mind-body awareness, sensing mind and body awareness emerges (*shadayatana*).
5. From sensing mind and body awareness, sensing and perceiving emerge (*spasha*).
6. From sensing and perceiving comes discriminating feelings (*vedana*).
7. From discriminating feelings, hunger and thirst emerge (*trishna*).
8. From hunger and thirst, craving and clinging emerge (*upadana*).
9. From craving and clinging conception emerges (*bhava*).

10. From conception, life emerges (*jeti*).
11. From life, aging, sickness, and death emerge (*jana-marana*).
12. From aging, sickness, and death, pain and suffering emerge.

Buddha explained: "In all these there is no doer and no one who benefits. They are empty phenomena and that is the way of the world. Empty phenomena have no maker, no god. They depend on their own conditions."

FIVE RULES OR PRECEPTS

Do not kill living beings, have loving kindness for them; give, do not take what is not yours, what is not freely given, and it is better to give than to receive; crave nothing and no one, be content with what you have; do not lie, slander, or speak harmfully -- speak kindly or be silent; and nothing in excess. But, be moderate.

FOUR INFINITE STATES OF MIND

Loving kindness; compassion; joy; letting go of material dependency.

THE FIVE DHYANA BUDDHAS (Tibetan)

Vairocana is the Central Dhyana Buddha whose color is white (all the colors), Dharmachakra wheel mudra, and his mantra is *Om*.

Aksobhya is the Dhyana Buddha of the East, blue color, Bhumisparsha consciousness mudra, and *Hum* is his mantra.

Ratnasambhava is the Dhyana Buddha of the South, yellow color, Verada openness mudra, and *Trah* or *Tram* is his mantra.

Amithaba is the Dhyana Buddha of the West, red color, Dhyana perception mudra, and *Hrih* mantra.

Amoghasiddhi is the Dhyana Buddha of the North, green color, Adhaya fearlessness mudra, and *Ah* mantra.

READINGS

1. A man wanted all his philosophical questions answered before he would follow the Buddha's teachings. Buddha said: "It is like being wounded by a poisoned arrow and you said to a physician: 'Do not remove the arrow until I learn the caste, birthplace, occupation, and motive of the person who wounded me.' You would die before you learned all that. So, saying 'I will not follow you until you answer all my questions, you would die before I could answer them" (*Majjhima Nikaya*).

2. King Milinda asked the Venerable Nagasena: "Where does wisdom dwell?" Nagasena replied: "Nowhere, O King." King Milinda said: "Then there is no such thing as wisdom." Nagasena asked: 'Where does the wind dwell, O King?" The King replied: "Nowhere." Then Nagasena said: "So, there is no such thing as wind" (*Milindapanha* 77).

3. Do not believe anything just because you heard it from a seeming authority. Do not believe in traditions just because they have been handed down for generations. Do not believe anything just because it is spoken by many. Do not believe anything just because it is in books. Do not believe anything based only on the authority of teachers or elders. Rather, after careful observation and analysis, you find what agrees with reason, is for good and benefits all, accept it and follow it. As the elephant endures the arrow, you should patiently bear with abuse because there are many unkind archers in the world (*Dhammapadda*).

4. Do not base views on knowledge, virtuous conduct, or religious observances. Avoid thinking that you are superior, inferior, or equal to others. The truly wise let go of the "self" and are free of attachments, do not depend on factual knowledge, do not dispute opinions, and are not set in any view. Those with no wish for either extreme of becoming or non-becoming, here or in any other existence, have no fixed view nor the least notion of views of anything seen, heard, or thought, and thus nothing influences them (*Sutta-nipata*).

5. As a rock is not moved by wind, the awakened are not moved by winds of praise or blame. They are as calm as a deep lake in still air because they are one with the Dharma (*Dhammapada* 6).

6. The bliss of a truth-seeking life is attainable by anyone who follows the path of unselfishness. If you cling to wealth it is better to throw it away than let it poison your heart. If you do not cling to it but use it wisely you will be a blessing to people. Wealth and power do not enslave; clinging to them enslaves (*Majjhima Nikaya*).

7. Be grateful to those who harm you; they help you to not do the same. Be grateful to those who deceive you; they teach you to be honest. Be grateful to those who abandon you; they help you find yourself. Be grateful to those who mislead you; they help you find your way. Be grateful to those who denounce you; they help deepen your insight and help you on the way to enlightenment (*Chin Kung,* Pure Land Buddhism).

SAYINGS

Words without meaning are like flowers without fragrance.
Words cannot measure what is immeasurable.
Searching lifts veil after veil. There are many veils.
Who asks errs; who answers errs, so it is often wise to
    say nothing.
Do not ask darkness to brighten, light to fade, or silence
    to speak. They cannot.
Awareness is like ripples from a far-off fountain.
We suffer from ourselves. We kiss the ever-turning wheel
    that runs over us.
Leave behind where you began whenever you begin.
As a Fletcher fashions straight arrows, the wise fashion
    their minds.
Whatever a hateful person can do to the hated, a wrongfully
    directed mind can do worse.
The forest of craving cannot be cleared by cutting down
    one tree.

BUDDHIST HOLIDAYS

Vesak (most celebrated): Buddha's birth day, the day of first
    full moon in May.
Dharma Day: Buddha's first sermon in The Deer Park, day
    of the first full moon in July.
Autumn Moon Festival, September at about the equinox.
Bodhi Day: Buddha leaving home at age 29, December 8 or
    the Sunday before.
Nirvana Day: Buddha's enlightenment, 2nd Sunday in February.
Sangha Day: Marks the 1250 who met with Buddha, day of the
    first moon, March.

TO LEARN MORE

Humphreys, C. (Ed) (1961). *The Wisdom of Buddhism.* New York: Random House.

MacHovec, F.J. (2007). *Divine spark: Spiritual intelligence in you and the universe.* www.lulu.com

MacHovec, F.J. (2007). *Light from the East, a gathering of Asian wisdom.* Berkeley CA: Stone Bridge Press.

2
TAO
Transcendent force

> Looked for, it cannot be seen.
> Reached for, it cannot be touched.
> Listened for it cannot be heard,
> Yet, Tao is everywhere.
>
> -- *Book of Tao*

Taoism is a nature philosophy and like Buddhism it became a religion. It emerged in the 5th century BCE about the same time as Buddhism but in China, not northern India. It had no connection to Buddhism until the 2nd century CE when it blended with it in northern India as **Dhyana Buddhism** that became **Ch'an Buddhism** in China and **Zen Buddhism** in Japan. The legendary author was **Lao-tse**, (say "louts"), **Lao-tzu** (Lao as "how" and "tzoo"), or **Li Erh** (ca 604-531 BCE, Chou dynasty) in Honan Province. The name means "old philosopher" or "old man" and he is pictured riding an ox. According to one legend, he was "the wisest man in all of China" and another says he was "keeper of the archives of China."

As for how the **Book of Tao** was written, it is said that at age 80 or 90, riding an ox to the mountains to die, the frontier guard recognized him and refused to let him pass because he had not left his wisdom to guide others. He sat and penned the 81 **sutras** (strands of thought or lessons) of the **Book of Tao**, left them, and continued on to the mountains never to be seen again. **Tao** (say "dow") means "way" or "transcending way"), **Te** or **Teh** means highest character or virtue, and Ching means book. So, **Tao Te Ching** means "book of the way and virtue or character."

The down side of Taoism is that over centuries of time as it became organized it was corrupted by superstition, charms, and rituals. Much the same happened to Buddhism as it spread to other nations and cultures, changed by local customs and traditions. But Buddha's **Four Noble Truths** and **8-fold Path** have not changed and, like the **Book of Tao**, reflect the same unchanging wisdom and insight could be called "the wisdom of the ages."

In this translation, the sutras are in two sections: those about **Tao** and those about **Teh** or **Te.** It is based on a comparative analysis of many previous translations but is gender-free, as LaoTse probably wrote it. We have no original, only copies of copies. Older versions use "sage" or "wise man," gender bias inconsistent with *mystic mother Yin* and *mystic father Yang*, equal in dynamic interaction. As you read the sutras let **the Tao** speak to you "according to its nature!" Here are all 81 sutras:

ABOUT TAO

IT IS ABSOLUTE AND ETERNAL

There is something mysterious, without beginning, without end, that existed before heaven and earth, silent, unchanging, and infinite. It is everywhere and it is inexhaustible. It is like a great mother of everything. I do not know its name but if I must name it I call it Tao. If I must describe it I call it supreme. Supreme is never-ending. Never-ending is far-reaching. Far-reaching means to eventually return. Tao is supreme, the universe is supreme, earth is supreme, and humanity is supreme. There are four supremes and humanity is one of them. Humanity is subject to the laws of the earth. The earth is subject to the laws of the universe. The universe is subject to the laws of Tao. Tao is subject only to the laws of its own nature (25).

IT IS BEYOND WORDS

The Tao described in words is not the real Tao. Names are useful but cannot describe Tao. It is the unnamed ultimate source of everything. Named, it is the great mother of everyone and everything. To see Tao, you must be without any selfish motive. With selfish motive only the surface is seen and not what is within. Those two observers are similar because they are both human, but differ very much in insight (1).

IT IS EVERYWHERE

Tao is so great it can be used to infinity. It is inexhaustible. Like nature, it is in all things and has been in all things from their beginnings. With it, sharp edges are rounded, differing angles intersect, various colors merge, and chaos is calmed. It is so deep its source is unknown and it is older even than thoughts of God (4).

SUPER-NATURAL

Tao is all-powerful, absolute, but it claims no title. Though incredibly simple and seemingly insignificant, the world has not understood it. If leaders used it everything would follow freely according to their nature. Heaven and earth would join and there would be peace with little effort. As civilization grew there was a need to name everything. With names it is wise to know when to stop. Knowing when to stop prevents harm. Tao is like a small stream that flows into rivers to the vast open sea (32).

THE GREATEST

Tao is everywhere, to the left and to the right. Everything is created from it. Nothing is rejected by it. Everything exists from it but it makes no claim to it. Without ulterior motive, it seems so insignificant. Being the source of everything it is truly great.

Because it does not claim greatness its greatness shines brightly (34).

LIKE A DRAWN BOW

Tao is like a drawn bow. The highest part is lowered and the lowest part is raised. Overall length is shortened and overall width is widened. Tao lowers the highest and raises the lowest but in the world the high are raised and the low are lowered. Who can take from the high and give to the low? Followers of Tao give without taking, achieve without claiming credit, and selflessly avoid recognition (77).

TAO IN THE HOME

You can know about the world without leaving home. You can see Tao in nature without looking closely. You can know it without scholarly study. The wise do not travel far to know Tao. They see without looking, know without studying, and achieve with little effort (47).

THE TAO PATH

Walk the path of Tao by avoiding bypaths of useless knowledge. The way of Tao is easy to follow but many prefer the bypaths. It is like palaces that are well kept but fields are untilled and storehouses empty. Being well dressed with expensive jewelry and swords, gorging with food and drink, having much money and property is excessive and invites crime. It is not the way of Tao (53).

WITHOUT TAO

Without Tao humanity and justice become official goals. When knowledge and wisdom become goals there is hypocrisy. When good parenting and obedient children are goals there is family discord. When loyalty is publicly praised there is inefficiency and corruption. When there is such darkness and disorder there is a need for great leaders (*18*).

EXISTENT NON-EXISTENCE

Looked for it cannot be seen. It is invisible. Listened for it cannot be heard. It is inaudible. Reached for, it cannot be touched. It is intangible. Though contradictory, these three are one. The outside is not bright. The inside is not dark. It is infinite, without beginning, without end. It is formless form, existent non-existence. It is elusive. Meet it and it has no face. Follow it and it has no back. Be one with it and you know true reality and are warmly welcomed into Tao (*14*).

VALUED NON-EXISTENCE

30 spokes join at the hub but using a wheel depends on the place where nothing exists. Clay is shaped into a vessel but its use depends on the inside where nothing exists. Doors and windows are set into walls but their use depends on spaces where nothing exists. So, there is value in using what can be seen, what exists, and value in using what cannot be seen, the non-existent (*11*).

TAO PROGRESS

Going forward in Tao seems like going backwards. Being open to it is the key to receiving it. Everything is produced from Tao yet its existence comes from non-existence (*40*).

A WIDE NET

Who is bold and evil is destructive and will be destroyed. Who is bold but good is supportive and they will be supported. Good and evil are in both kinds of boldness but Tao flows only to one. Even followers of Tao may have difficulty with this.

Tao is not contentious but is subject to contention. It has no voice but its message can be heard clearly. It does not command attention but it attracts attention. It is a wide net from which nothing is lost (73).

CONTENT CONTENTMENT

If the world followed Tao thoroughbred horses would work the farms. When the world forsakes Tao cavalry horses graze in the parks. Discontent is a great weakness. Greed is a great sin. Ruthless ambition is a great defect. Be content with contentment, with just enough, and you will be at peace (46).

SEEMS FOOLISH

When the world thinks that Tao is great, it is great in a different way. It is in the difference that it is great. If it were like anything else, it would mot be great. There are three special treasures of Tao to cherish and preserve. The first is love, without it nothing is possible. The second is moderation, the mystic balance. The third is humility, to know you come from nothing and return to nothing. Without these special treasures there is darkness. Love is so strong it conquers. There is no defense against it. Tao arms with love those open to it (67).

ABOUT TEH

TEH IN TAO

Tao generates and energizes everything and Teh sustains it. Tao is all-powerful and Teh is all-sustaining. Tao and Teh flow naturally in everyone and everything. They nurture and protect. They cultivate and comfort, productive but not possessive. They dominate and they recede. In leaders, it is hidden Teh (51).

SCOPE OF TEH

What is firmly planted is not easily uprooted. What is firmly held is not easily lost. In this way generation follows generation. Be open to Tao and Teh will be there. Open families to Tao and Teh is there. Open the city to Tao and Teh flows. Open the nation to Tao and Teh grows. Open the world to Tao and Teh is world-wide. In this way, Teh is a measure of one's self, family, city, state, and nation. You can know this by seeing it in action (54).

SEEN AND UNSEEN TEH

Teh flows from Tao. Tao flows from nature, invisible, intangible, obscure. It is invisible but it can be perceived. It is intangible but it can be felt. It is obscure but it can be understood. The basic life force is in it. This has been true and self-evident since ancient times. Realize it by these signs and what is within you (21).

ANCIENT TEH

The ancient followers of Tao were wise, subtle, and profound. They understood so deeply they themselves were misunderstood. They were not easily recognized, so their strength was undiminished. They were cautious like crossing a frozen stream in midwinter, alert like traveling through a strange land, unassuming as melting ice, as dignified as an honored guest, receptive as a valley, and friendly as freely mixing muddy water. Who can make sense of a world as clouded as muddy water? Left alone it would clear itself. Can such stillness remain? Agitate it and it becomes cloudy again. Act selflessly with Tao and there is movement without clouding of selfish motives. Hardship can be endured as movement continues (15).

TEH KNOWING

Who knows says nothing. Who speaks does not know. Stop the senses. Do not puzzle over their questions as you undo their tangles. Be one with the light to better see the ways of the world. This is mystic unity beyond accepting or rejecting, risk or benefit, better or worse, therefore a valuable treasure (56)

MORE FROM LESS

When the truly wise see Tao they seek it more. When others see Tao they are content to look no further. Those who do not see it laugh at it. If it were not laughed at it would not be Tao. Tao enlightenment can seem dull, progress like regress, and the straight path crooked. Having Teh can seem lowly like a valley or tarnished metal. Strong Teh can seem weak, sufficient Teh insufficient, and supportive Teh can seem frail. Great space has no edges or corners. Great form can be formless. Great ability is limitless. Great music can be uplifting. Tao is like that, hidden, formless, yet energizing and uplifting everything (41).

WORDS, FACTS, AND ACTS

Words of truth are not necessarily impressive. Impressive words are not necessarily true. Who has Teh has no need to argue. Who argues does not have Teh. Who has Teh does not study trivial facts. Who studies trivial facts does not have Teh.

Those with Teh fulfill life for others and are therefore full of life, give freely of themselves and are therefore wealthy. Tao serves absolutely and those with Teh serve selflessly (*81*).

TEH STRENGTH

It is wise to know others but wiser to first know yourself. To master others is a strength but to master yourself is greater strength. The wise are content with just enough and are therefore self-sufficient. They move with just enough speed and therefore are well motivated. They are natural and sincere, so they endure. They are remembered and so are immortal (*33*).

LESS IS MORE

Which is more important, that the world know you or that you know your-self? Which is more valuable, money or your mind? Which leads to greater evil, winning or losing? Strong attachments and great wealth risk loss. Being content with just enough prevents extremes. Know when you have enough and there is less to lose. Know when to stop and there is less danger. Realizing this is to endure (*44*).

HAVE AND HAVE NOT

Who has Teh does not boast of it, a sign of really having it. Those who boast of it do not have it. Teh is selfless, and the highest morality is also selfless. Public morals make claims and can lead to selfish motives. Custom and tradition make claims and can also lead to selfish motives. Without Tao, public morals are the rule. With them wellbeing becomes the rule. Without public wellbeing, conformity becomes the rule. Without conformity laws and regulations become the rule. There is disorder and confusion. Followers of Tao endure because they focus on deeper truth that is below the surface, what is inside. They are receptive to one and not the other (*38*).

WATER MOTIVE

The highest motive is to be like water. Water is essential to life but it never demands a fee or proclaims its importance. Instead, it flows humbly to the lowest level and so is much like Tao. In their homes the wise love the land, the ground on which homes are built. In their hearts they love what is natural and genuine. In their friendships they are caring and giving. In their talk they are sincere. In governing they act in good faith and good will. In their work they are reliable and quietly efficient. Their goal is selfless serenity, a sign of Tao, and with it there is no strife (8).

WATER POWER

There is nothing humbler or more yielding than water yet it can wear down what is strong and rigid. There is nothing like it. The weak can overpower the strong. The flexible can overcome the rigid. Everyone can see this but few use it. The truly wise know to lead a nation they need to humble themselves to that nation. Who bears the sins of the world is fit to lead the world. This truth can seem illogical (78).

ETERNAL CONSTANT

Open yourself and realize inner harmony. Be one with everyone and everything. If distracted, return to nature which restores inner harmony. Finding inner harmony helps realize your destiny. Realizing your destiny opens you to the eternal constant. Knowing the eternal constant opens you to great wisdom. Not realizing these is a great misfortune. You must be unbiased. Being unbiased is to return to nature. Returning to nature is like Tao. What is like Tao endures free of harm (16).

SPARE YOUR TALK

Nature is sparing in its talk. An unusually strong wind or heavy rain seldom last long. And where do they originate? In nature. If nature is so sparing in its talk how much more should you be? Follow Tao and Tao will follow you. Follow Teh and Teh will follow you. Fail to follow them and you will fail. Follow nothing and nothing will follow you. Welcome Tao and Tao will welcome you. Welcome Teh and Teh will welcome you. Ignore them and they will ignore you. Have no trust and no one will trust you (23).

MOVING ON

What is still is easily held. What is unimportant is easy to anticipate. What is rigid can easily be broken. What is small can easily be moved. Cope with problems early before they grow. A still mind is difficult to upset. A tree with an arm's girth of trunk grows from a tiny sprout. A 9-storied terrace begins with one clump of dirt. A journey of 1000 miles begins with the first step. Overdoing can undo. Over-reaching can lose hold. The wise do not overdo so they do not undo anything. They do not over-reach so they are never out of touch. Failure can occur close to success. Be as careful at the end as at the beginning. The wise value what is not valued. They do not long for what they do not have. They unlearn what was learned. They seek what was lost. They help everyone and everything follow nature and their own nature without interfering (64).

GOOD IN EVIL

Tao is at the source of everything, treasure for the good and refuge for the bad. High sounding words and deeds can be used for evil. Why reject them? At the crowning of leaders it is better to give the gift of Tao rather than jade and prize horses. Why did the ancients value Tao? It is because the good who seek it will find it and the evil who find it can be forgiven. So, Tao is a treasure for everyone (62).

POSITIVE INDIFFERENCE

Nature is indifferent to life. Every-one and everything is treated like a sacrificial straw dog. The wise are indifferent in the same way, realizing humanity is like a straw dog and the universe is like a bellows that empties as it fills. They proceed as they recede and produce as they are reduced. It is beyond words and futile to try to describe it further (5).

TEH SECURITY

Having Teh is like a child poisonous insects and snakes do not bite and predatory animals and wild birds do not attack. Hands are weak but can grasp firmly. Too young to work but growing up in good health. Too young to speak but they freely voice their feelings. This requires inner harmony. Having inner harmony is to know the eternal. To know the eternal is to be truly wise. Disharmony upsets everything and interferes with nature. It is not the way of Tao. Whatever is not the way of Tao cannot last (55).

DOUBLE ENLIGHTENMENT

Good roads have no barriers. Good speakers are not misunderstood. Good planning needs no detailed notes. Good security does not rely only on locks or fences. Good knots hold but are easily untied. The wise are good because they are good to others. No one is rejected. They help without reservation. This is double enlightenment. So, the good are lessons for the bad. Those who are not good are lessons for the good. Who does not value such teachers and students are misguided, even if they are intelligent. This is subtle wisdom (27).

TEH TRUST

The truly wise are selfless. People's needs are their needs. The good are treated with goodness. Those who are not good are also treated with goodness. This is the goodness of Tao. They trust those who trust them. They also trust those who do not trust them. This is the trust of Tao. The truly wise accept the world impartially and in good faith and people remain themselves. Like innocent children the wise accept everyone as members of one family (49).

LIFE IN DEATH

Life leaves when death arrives. There are 13 parts of living and dying, four limbs and nine openings. Why? Because living tips the balance toward dying. Those who know this are safe from the horns of the wild buffalo and the claws of the tiger. Weapons of war find no target. Why? Because it is not yet time for death (50).

MISSED UNDERSTANDING

My message is easily understood and put into practice. The world does not understand it or put it into practice. My words have an ancient source and my actions have meaningful purpose. When this is not understood I am not understood. The few who understand are better for it, proof there is value in what I say and do. It is best to wear common clothes and carry valuables in your heart (70).

SIMILAR DIFFERENCES

To value only beauty is in itself a kind of ugliness. To value only good is in itself a kind of evil. Opposites share the same basic energy. Existence and non-existence differ in cause and effect. Easy and difficult differ by degree. Near and far differ in distance. Low and high differ in height. Shrill and deep differ in tone. Before and after differ in time. The truly wise accept this and work despite differences or differing words. They teach by example rather than by words. They accept everything and reject nothing. They are productive and not possessive, freely sharing what they do. They achieve without claiming credit. Their achievements are self-evident and can never be taken away (2).

DANGEROUS EXTREMES

There is a danger in extremes. Pull a bowstring too far and you wish you had let go before. Hone a sword blade too well and it wears too soon. Fill your house with jade and gold and you invite thieves. Be proud or arrogant and you hasten your own failure. Reach goals and be satisfied to go no further. This is the way of Tao (9)

RISK OF EXTREMES

Stand on tiptoe and you are unsteady. Walk with long strides and you cannot long keep up the pace. Make a show of yourself and you cannot really shine. Seek only glory and you cannot be the best leader. Be self-righteous and you lose the respect of the people. Be self-centered and you lose the love of the people. In Tao these are excessive and inappropriate and even in worldly matters should be avoided and those who follow Tao avoid them (24).

AVOID EXTREMES

Who tries to win the world loses it. The world is sacred and beyond reach. Trying to seize it interferes with nature. According to the Tao, some things proceed but others recede, some move rapidly, others slowly, some succeed with strength, others with weakness, and some are active and others passive. So, the wise avoid excess, extremes, and exaggeration (29).

YIN-YANG

To have mystic Yang and also to have mystic Yin is like a stream that flows through the world. Being like that stream is to have constant Teh like the innocence of a child. Having the light of Yang but also the shade of Yin achieves a high standard. Having that high standard is Teh connecting with Tao. To achieve yet be humble is like a fountain to the world that reaches high yet flows to the lowest level. Being like that fountain is to have mystic unity. Divide mystic unity. Its parts become tools. In the hands of the wise those tools are means to an end, never ends in themselves, all part of Tao (*28*).

UNIFYING BALANCE

In Tao there is unity. Unity is the source duality. Duality is the source of triples. Triples are the source of everything. The shade of mystic Yin is on the back of everything and the light of mystic Yang is on the front of everything. Balance comes from their interaction, like breathing in and out. Being alone and unwanted is fearful but even the best leaders experience it. Losing can be beneficial. Winning can be harmful. A major teaching many have said before: the violent come to violent ends (*42*).

MOTIVELESS YIN

Tao never acts directly yet it is indirectly in everything. If leaders followed this example, everything would improve naturally and selfish motives would become selflessly simple. With selfless simplicity there is no need to compete. With no competing there is harmony and all is well in the world (*37*).

MYSTIC MOTHER YIN

Yin is the mystic mother, every-where, even at the source of heaven and earth. Thinly veiled and delicately formed, find her and let her help you. She is infinite and inexhaustible (6).

VIRTUE OF A FOOL

Stop amassing trivial knowledge and you will be less burdened. What is the difference between disagreement and agreement, beauty and ugliness, fear or being feared? Such nonsense never ends. Others seem happy as if at a feast or celebration but I alone are as aloof as a newborn baby too young to be so happy. Others seem to have more than they need but I alone am content with less. Others seem knowledgeable and bright but I alone seem uninformed and dull. Others seem to see things clearly but I alone seem to be in the dark. Others seem are clever and quick-witted but I alone am unsettled as a vast ocean and aimless as still air. Others seem to settle down but I alone choose different places. It is as if I am sustained by a mystic mother (20).

MYSTIC VIRTUE

Can you keep mind and spirit on the path of Tao? Can you breathe softly and gently like a newborn baby? Can you purify yourself to perfection? Can you love and lead without self-interest? Can you be the receptive mystic Yin beginning to end without weakening? Find your way knowing nothing? Be productive and supportive to others without being posses-sive. Give freely of yourself without obligating others. Help without getting in the way. This is a mystic virtue (10).

QUIET STRENGTH

That which decreases first increases. That which weakens first strengthens. That which is rejected is first accepted. That which is taken must first be given. The flexible overcomes the inflexible. Being gentle overcomes strength. Strength is best kept hidden, like fish swimming under water. This is subtle wisdom (36).

SOFT-HARD STRENGTH

What is soft can penetrate what is hard. What is existent can permeate what is non-existent. There is advantage in working quietly and taking no action. Few actions are as useful as silence and working quietly. Few know this (43).

INNER-EXTERNAL NEEDS

Colors can flood the eye, sound can deafen the ear, and taste can overpower the tongue. In like manner, thoughts and feelings can unbalance the mind. Selfish striving can interfere with a good life. The wise satisfy their inner needs and avoid satisfying external needs selfishly. They accept   one and avoid the other (12).

SERENE BALANCE

A great achievement that seems a failure does not lessen its value. What is full can seem empty but does not lessen its usefulness. What is straight can seem crooked, great skill can seem awkward, and the most eloquent can seem boring. Moving soothes feeling cold, resting soothes being over-heated, and sharing and peace soothe a troubled world (45).

FLEX!

Newborn infants are soft, yielding. The dead are hard, unyielding. Living plants are soft and pliant. Dead, they are withered and brittle. Being hard, unyielding, withered, or brittle is like death. Being yielding, soft, or pliant is like being fully alive. So, a headstrong army will lose just as an unyielding tree snaps from the axe. The place of the rigid is below. The place of the flexible is above (76).

YIELDING STRENGTH

Bend and you will not break. Yield and you remain whole. Empty yourself and you will be filled. Grow up and you will not grow old. Have little and you have enough. Have too much and you will be needy. Therefore, the truly wise seek and hold close Mystic Unity. They are good examples to all. They do not seek recognition and so they are worthy of recognition. They do not boast, so they are worthy of praise. They earn trust by trusting others. They lead well by not seeking to control. They win by not competing selfishly. The old saying is true: "Bend and you will not break; yield and you will remain whole" (22).

LEARN LESS, MORE

The world's way of knowledge is to learn more and more every day. The way of Tao is to learn less and less every day. Seeking trivial knowledge lessens inner peace. Find and master the indirect way and all will go well. The world belongs to those who let go of it. Try to control it and it is already beyond reach (48).

FORTUNE-MISFORTUNE

Good fortune and misfortune can both cause problems. High and low feelings can co-exist. How? Good fortune raises and misfortune lowers. There is anxiety with both. Be selfless and there is no anxiety. Those who try to better the world are worthy to lead the world. Those who love people are worthy to be loved by people (13).

KNOW YOU DON'T KNOW

It is best to know that you don't know. Not knowing this is sick. The wise realize this and so they are not sick. But, they are sick of knowing what is not worth knowing (71).

THE ROPE OF TAO

Do not boast of your wisdom. Avoid trivial knowledge. Everyone benefits. Avoid proclaiming justice and humanity and there will be more responsibility and caring. Avoid overabundance and there will be less crime. These three avoidances are strands braided into the strong rope of Tao, strongest when tied to a pure mind, simplicity, selflessness, and restraint (19).

SELFLESS POWER

Heaven and earth endure because they do not exist for themselves alone. The truly wise are like that. They choose to be last and so they are worthy to be first. They empty themselves and so they are fulfilled. They are selfless and so they fully realize their true selves (7).

MOTHER-CHILD SERENITY

The world's beginning was like a mother giving birth. Know the mother and you can know her children. Know her children and you can remain close to their mother. Live this way and there will be no fear of life or death. Eyes and mouth closed, life has few problems. Eyes and mouth open, life has more problems. Accept weakness to overcome weakness. Use inner light to increase enlightenment. This is the way of Tao (52).

HEAVY-LIGHT STRENGTH

Heaviness can overpower lightness. Serenity can overpower restlessness. The truly wise travel lightly but keep their heavy baggage close by. Though there are many sights to see away from home, they are happy to stay home. Should a leader of 10,000 chariots be heavy or light? Regard everything lightly and you may lose sight of deeper truths. Be deeply troubled and you may lose yourself (26).

YIN-YANG LEADERS

The world will follow without fear, serene and secure, a leader who holds close the great Yin Yang. Passing strangers stop for music and tasty food, not for the words of Tao that seem to them unappealing and meaningless. Look for it and you cannot see it. Listen for it and you cannot hear it. Use it and it is inexhaustible (35).

BEST LEADERS

The best leaders are inconspicuous. The next best are respected. The next are feared. The next are defied. If you do not trust people, people will not trust you. The wise are humble and soft-spoken. When the best leader's work is done and goals are achieved, people say: "Look what we did" (17).

LOWLY HIGH LEADERSHIP

Why do rivers and seas overflow lowlands? It is because they lower themselves. And so, to be elevated by people lower yourself to them. To lead, walk behind. The wise are above but no one feels their weight. They lead but no one feels blocked. They do not quarrel so no one quarrels with them. They are not aggressive, so no one is aggressive to them. The world would respect and never tire of such leaders (66).

LEAD HUMBLY

Mystic unity makes the heavens constant, the earth stable, and valleys fertile. It uplifts the spirit. It brings everything into existence and success to the best leaders. Without it the heavens would not be constant, the earth would be unstable and valleys infertile. Without it, human spirit would falter. Without it, the best leaders would fail. What is high depends on what is low, as a chariot depends on its many parts, moving or still. So, the best leaders rely on everyone and everything. It is better to be as coarse and plain as a stone than polished fine jade (39).

NORMAL-ABNORMAL

Lead indirectly and quietly and the people are happy. Lead loudly and aggressively and people are unhappy. Happy and unhappy are opposites. Why? What is normal? Normal can become abnormal. What looks good can become evil. It is confusing. The truly wise are square but are without sharp corners. They can be pointed but not painful. They can wedge in or out but without sharp angles. They are bright but not blinding (58).

LEAD WITH MODERATION

Moderation is an important skill. It is to yield but with strength. With that kind of strength anything is possible. When anything is possible there are no limits. Without limits power is limitless, a mother principle. Be one with it and your leadership will endure because it will be firmly rooted in Tao (59).

HARMLESS LEADERSHIP

Lead as you would cook a small fish, careful not to overdo it. Lead with the strength of Tao and evil weakens. Evil may continue but with less harm. When evil is less harmful leaders are also less harmful. Then, neither leaders nor evil are harmful, no one is harmed, and everyone benefits (60).

PREVENT EVIL EXCESS

Do not encourage competition and there will be less rivalry and malice. Do not encourage wealth and there will be less theft. Do not encourage abundance. There will be less harmful excess. Wise leaders encourage emptying to fulfill and weakening craving to strengthen character. Without cunning and selfishness those who are cunning and selfish can do no harm. Lead with restraint and all will be well (3).

MOVE GRACIOUSLY

When people lose respect for leaders it is time for change. Do not crowd them and there will be more room in which to move. Do not reject them and they will not reject you. So, be yourself but with restraint. Accept yourself without undue pride. Cultivate what is inside, not just what is outside (72).

SIMPLICITY

Ancient followers of Tao did not use it to enlighten others but to increase simplicity and decrease useless trivia. Leadership is difficult when people value useless trivia. Lead with useless trivia and you are the people's enemy. Lead without useless trivia and you are the people's blessing. Understand this and you understand mystic Teh. It is far-reaching and it returns with greater strength and harmony (65).

ACHIEVE INDIRECTLY

Achieve indirectly and with quiet efficiency. Savor the tasteless. Raise the lowly. Consider the few as many. Respond kindly to unkindness. Resolve what is difficult while it is easy, the complex while it is simple. The world's major problems can be solved while they are minor. The hardest work can be done with less effort. The truly wise do not actively seek greatness so greatness comes easily to them. A promise lightly made is difficult to keep. See everything as easy and everything can become difficult. The wise know what is difficult, therefore they have few difficulties (63).

HEALING TEH

There is seldom complete healing after severe injury. By settling a heated dispute some hatred is left behind. How can this be prevented? Those with Teh defend the weak and do not seek vengeance. Those without Teh attack the weak and seek vengeance. Those with Teh do their duty. Those without Teh let others do their duty. There is equality in Tao. Goodness freely flows through it for the good of all (79).

WHY PEOPLE SUFFER

People suffer when taxes are high. That is why they suffer. People resist leaders who are oppressive. That is why they resist. People do not fear death when leaders prize their own lives more. That is why people do not fear death. Those who do not interfere with life gain more from life (75).

SMALL IS GREAT

An ideal organization or state is small, with few people. It has machines and tools but little need for them. It has vehicles but no need to travel far. It has weapons but no need to brandish them. The people so love it there they do not leave. They are satisfied with simple knotted ropes for counting, simple food and clothing, modest homes, and simple customs. Other organizations and states are wary of one another. People in the ideal state hear roosters crowing and dogs barking from other places but they   are content living where they are (80).

GREATER IS LESSER

A great nation is like land where streams descend. It is a where mystic Yin meets, quiet, unpretentious. With gracious receptivity it subdues mystic Yang. A great nation lowers itself to a smaller nation and thus merits its support. The smaller nation lowers itself to the greater nation and in so doing merits its support. So, whatever is low is worthy of support. Great and lower nations need such people. When both kinds of nations meet their needs, the greater nation should still be supportive (*61*).

SELFLESSNESS SECRET

Skilled leaders are not aggressive. Skilled warriors do not lose self-control. A winning strategy is to never antagonize the enemy. The best way to lead others is to share equally with them and adapt to them. It is the secret of selflessness and it is to be one with ancient Tao (*68*).

BE LAWFUL NOT FULL OF LAWS

Lead doing what is right. Wage war by clever strategy. To control the world, let go of it. How do I know? Many rules weaken order. Many weapons invite trouble. Many crafty people mean more wrongdoing. Many strict laws mean more offenses. The wise simplify, so people understand, restrained, so people are content. They are selfless, so people's lives are enriched. Being un-selfish is the simplicity of uncarved wood (57).

WAR IS NOT TAO

Weapons of war invite war and the followers of Tao avoid using them. Teh leadership favors peace. Leaders who are without Teh favor war. When war cannot be avoided, weapons are used only when necessary. The best policy is restraint because there is no joy in war. To find joy in it is to delight in violence. Peace brings happiness. War brings sadness. Who delights in violence is not fit to lead. In war, the commanders officiate at many funerals. The grief of both sides should be shared, even in victory (*31*).

WHEN WAR IS INEVITABLE

Followers of Tao counsel leaders against using force. Force can backfire. Thorn bushes grow when armies march. Bad times follow. The need to protect should never be for selfish reasons. Achieve victory then stop, without pride, boasting, flaunting superiority, or indulging in the spoils. Instead, regret not preventing war because it is not good to conquer by force. Overdoing invites decline. It is not the way of Tao and what departs from Tao cannot long endure (*30*).

SECRET WEAPON

Military strategists would rather defend than attack, and retreat a foot rather than advance an inch. Doing so is like marching in place but not really going anywhere. It is to seem un-prepared, but actually ready. This is winning with passivity. It is a secret weapon. There is no error more tragic than underestimating the enemy. It risks losing everything. When evenly matched armies battle, the passive side is more likely to win (*69*).

CAPITAL PUNISHMENT WARNING

When people do not fear death why threaten them with it? When people fear death they are threatened by it. Who then wants to be executioner? There is only one supreme executioner. To assume that role is like giving unskilled workers the axe of a master carpenter. They could chop off their own hands (*74*).

LAO'S LAST WORDS?

We have no record of any last words of *LaoTse* but *Sutra* 67 could well be what he would have said:

I leave you with three jewels. Guard them and keep them safe. The first is love, to know that living is giving, everyone is brother and sister, and the one great law of life is love. Without it nothing is possible. The second is moderation, to know the mystic balance, avoid extremes and accept differences as ways to grow. The third is humility, to know you are born with nothing and die with nothing, but to die and be remembered is to have immortality (*67, edited*).

TAI CHI CHUAN

T'ai Chi Ch'uan or **Taijiquan** means "supreme ultimate or boundless fist." It is an internal "soft style" martial art some say is applied Taoism. There are different styles though most are based on the Chen family system taught to the Yang family in 1820 CE. The similarities across styles suggest a common origin. "Hard" martial arts use tense muscles but Tai Chi uses relaxed muscles, emphasizing balance in self and others, and applying this mentally and physically. An attack is neutralized by relaxed leverage.   Slow, repetitive work increases circulation and reduces stress.   Students learn defensive skills first. Loving kindness is emphasized as mercy to opponents: "I would rather maim than kill, hurt than maim, intimidate than hurt, and avoid than intimidate" (Shaolin temple).

The underlying philosophy is in Taoism's **Yin** mystic mother and **Yang** mystic father forces in dynamic interaction. The underlying principle is as reflected in the **Book of Tao**: "From ultimate softness comes ultimate hardness." Tai Chi training begins with slow solo *ch'uan* movement for straight spine, relaxed breathing, and natural range of motion, then *t'ui shou push-hands* "sensitive sticking" with a partner to develop reflexes and leverage and learn timing, coordination, and interaction.

T'ai Chi Ch'uan is still taught as a martial art by traditional practitioners but is more popular worldwide to maintain optimal health as *moving meditation.* Traditional Tai Chi training uses solo and 2-person routines and acupressure manipulation.

In a fight, using hardness to resist can injure both persons. Collision of yang with yang is *double-weighted* and the ideal is to receive incoming force with softness, "sticking" with it and following it until it exhausts itself. In the **Book of Tao**: "What is soft and pliable defeats the hard and strong." Alert calm helps develop sensitivity. Pushes and strikes with open hand, fingers, fist, palm, wrist, forearm, elbow, shoulder, back, hip, knee, and feet, to eyes, throat, heart, groin, or acupressure points.

Five major styles are named for the Chinese families that originated them. In order of popularity: **Yang, Wu, Chen, Sun,** and **Wu/Hao.** There are many new styles but the best known is **Wu Tang** "original style" of 12th century monk Zhang Sanfeng at Wu Tang Shan monastery, a center for martial arts. It is said he learned **Tao Yin** (*Pinyin daoyin*) breathing from Taoists and martial arts from Buddhists at Shaolin monastery. He combined them in **T'ai Chi Ch'uan.** So, like Zen, Tai Chi is a blend of Buddhism and Taoism.

There is no universal certification. Anyone can learn the moves and teach them. Many teachers left China during the Cultural Revolution. In 1956, China sponsored a Committee that met with four wushu teachers to formulate the 24-posture *Yang family hand form* simpler than longer 88 to 108 classic solo forms. In 1976 a *combined 48 form* was developed with features of **Ch'en, Yang, Wu,** and **Sun.**

Shorter forms do not include as much conditioning and are used mainly in six minute competition. The *42-form wushu* was used in the 1990 Asian Games. But, traditional **Tai Chi** families do *not* teach Sports Committee forms which they see as only for sport, not a martial art, lack higher standards, quality control by masters, and martial arts applications.

Tai Chi is useful as a healthy exercise and physical therapy, confirmed by many research studies.

K'UNG FU-TSE (Confucius)

Confucianism competed with Taoism in China and, being a more passive nature philosophy, was not as popular. The name *Confucius* is Latinized English for K'ung FuTse (c. 551-479 BCE), an administrator who emphasized social and ceremonial behavior more than spiritual development. Today, he would be a management consultant! Confucianism, unlike Taoism, is more concrete than abstract, more social than spiritual and metaphysical.

The *Analects of Confucius* are actually a collection of writings and sayings attributed to K'ung FuTse, but it is unlikely he wrote all of them. He did not give his sources. It is suspected zealous followers edited what he wrote and sometimes added material they thought he would have said or what was needed at the time.

K'ung FuTse was a Mandarin. That name projects an image of propriety, civic and filial duty. He saw the ideal society as orderly and appropriate behavior as a duty. This contributed to the proverbial Asian "save face" social interaction. Confucian male-dominated society required loyalty to the emperor, rulers, and fathers. Wives, daughters, and sisters were subservient. Until the mid-12th century the *Analects* were valued as ancient teachings. The Sung Sages used them as a basal textbook in schools. They were used as the basis for China's civil service examinations.

Examples of appropriate conduct: men should walk on the right, women on the left; friends do not overtake one another going the same way; gray-haired persons carry things in only one hand; younger children walk behind the older "as geese follow one another in a row;" children who come upon teachers should stand with arms crossed on their chest and speak only if spoken to.

In the *Analects*, K'ung FuTse included some personal information:

> I have transmitted what I was taught without adding anything of my own. I do not have innate knowledge. I love the past and I have diligently investigated it.

> You are mistaken if you see me as one who seeks to learn and preserve as much as possible. I have only one thread and on it I string every-thing.

Emphasis on public ceremonies:

> Why have ceremonies? To have an orderly society, and should be done correctly and well according to established rules. Not doing so is like a blind man groping about without help, or finding one's way in a dark room without light. Ceremonies are like riverbanks that prevent floods. Do away with riverbanks and there is destructive flooding. Do away with ceremonies and there will be confusion and disorder.

On everyday behavior:

> Anyone who enters with a guest yields at every door. At the innermost door, beg leave to enter first to arrange seating. The guest enters after bowing repeatedly and declining to enter. Guests enter the door to the left. The host enters the door to the right. If there are steps, guests should walk up the west side and the host should walk up the east side.

More social rules:

> Open doors are to be left open, closed doors
> remain closed; eyes downcast when entering a room
> with arms raised as if listening intently and without
> turning to one side or the other; anyone twice as old
> is treated as father, older than 10 years as an older
> brother, five years older as an equal but walked
> behind; children hold an elder's hand with both
> their hands facing in the same direction.

Much in the *Analects* describes goals of personal development, what K'ung FuTse called "being a superior man" or "gentleman." The following excerpts are rendered gender-free, superior or wise *person* rather than *man* or *gentleman* (K'ung FuTse probably would not approve):

> The ancients shared similar virtues. To manage
> their states well they managed families well. To
> manage families well they cultivated character.
> To cultivate character they learned to think more
> clearly. To think clearly they managed feelings better.
> To manage feelings better they were sincere. Being
> sincere increased their awareness. With increased
> awareness they studied things more closely. Studying
> things closely increased knowledge and awareness,
> sincerity, thinking clearly, and character. With these,
> families and states were better managed and there
> was peace and happiness throughout the empire.

> A superior person is resolute in firmness, though
> not rigidly so, seeks to do what is right not what is
> easy, is accepting not rejecting, dignified not vain,
> sociable not clannish, articulate not antagonistic. A
> superior person uses nine thoughtful considerations:
> eyes see what is there, ears hear what is said, faces

benign, conduct respectful, words sincere, in business, efficient and if in doubt consults others, if angry is aware of the possible effect, faced with opportunity, he thinks how to use it well. Archers who miss the target do not look elsewhere for the cause. They look for the cause in themselves.

Nine useful rules: cultivate yourself; honor others of talent and virtue; show affection to your family; respect superiors; be kind to others; relate to subordinates as your own children; encourage creativity and innovation; be fair despite distance; and honor distinguished leaders.

Let virtue be a higher goal than power or status, strength of character more than any other challenge, and wisdom more than material gain. Do this and you are less likely to fail. To find and fulfill yourself help others to find and fulfill themselves.

A master answers questions like ringing a bell. A bell struck lightly is the small sound in an answer to simple questions. A bell struck harder is the louder sound of deeper questions. A master's answer is like a bell struck with full resonant sound appropriate to the question

An administrator, K'ung FuTse gave practical advice:
When personal conduct is good there is little need to issue orders. Everyone behaves properly. When personal conduct is not good there is a greater need to issue orders and fewer people will obey them. Govern with five strengths: be generous not   extravagant; assign tasks fairly; pursue goals without greed; be dignified not vain; be firm but friendly."

3
ZEN MIND

**Do not get entangled with
any object but stand above,
move on, and be free.**
-- Rinzai Zen saying

Zen Buddhism is the Japanese variation of China's **Ch'an Buddhism** which evolved from **Dhyana Buddhism**, founded by Seng Tien in northern India ca 2d-3rd century CE. He blended Taoism with Buddhism. *Dhyana* is Sanskrit for contemplation or wisdom. Bodhidharma (420-530 CE), "the blue-eyed monk," spread it to China as **Ch'an Buddhism** (Chinese for *dhyana*). Centuries later it spread to Japan as **Zen Buddhism** (*dhyana* in Japanese).

Bodidharma was the 1st Chinese Patriarch, 28th Patriarch of India, and a king's son. He received the mind-seal from 27th Patriarch Prajnatar by realizing pure mind-nature or Buddha-mind. He left India, crossed the Himalayas, settled in northern China and spent nine years in a cave meditating. He taught **direct pointing,** a system of direct enlightenment and is also credited with developing **kung fu.**

From northern India to China, Japan, and other nations the movement continued to evolve into separate sects, though only **Rinzai** and **Soto** survived, though Soto was more popular and influential. Here is a brief history:

Linji-zong (Chinese, **Rinzai-shu** in Japanese) was founded by Linji Yixuan in China during the Tang Dynasty (618-917 CE), the golden age of China. Hui-neng (638-713 CE), 6th Chinese Patriarch, stressed the need to realize the inherent pure mind or Buddha-mind, the only true human nature and original mind of a newborn baby, alone or with help. From his **Platform Sutra:**

It is by our own innate wisdom that we enlighten ourselves, and so help from a learned friend is of no use if there is delusion by false dharma and wrong views. Wrong views are eliminated instantly by prajna wisdom. Realizing the pure Buddha-mind attains Nirvana. Our tradition is thoughtlessness, our basis is non-objectivity, its feature is non-attachment in the pure   mind-nature, and our goal is idealessness, free of delusion in a mind aloof.

Myoan Eisai (1141-1215 CE) or Eisai Zenji brought **Linji-zong** to Japan in 1191. Met with strong opposition in Kyoto by the Buddhist establishment, he traveled to Kamakura where the Shogun and Samurai were more receptive. In fact, they included **Rinzai-shu** in Samurai training. Some criticized it as weakening Buddhism by adding martial arts. Rinzai seeks enlightenment by **satori** using **koans** and parables to bypass the intellect, shock the mind ("shatter the dish"), and to "overcome word drunkenness" with a state of meditative awareness.

Martial arts are often included, possibly a result of the earlier Samurai connection. **Koans** have no single right answer, but many appropriate answers. Parables are used to impart dhyana imagery. The goal is to *experience* and not *think,* and to *let everything be.* **Rinzai** declined in the 18th century until Hakuin Ekaku revived it. **Soto** has been more popular. Old Japanese saying: "Rinzai for Shogun, Soto for peasants." Eisai also brought tea from China to Japan. In the 15th century Ikkyu introduced the tea ceremony into Japanese culture.

Caodong-zong (Chinese, **Soto** in Japan) came to Japan by Dogen Zenji (1200-1253 CE). It is one of three schools that developed from **Shih-T'ou Hsi-chien** in China (700-790 CE, **Sekito Kisen** Japanese) in the mountains of Hunan province. Dogen was trained at Mt. Hiei but said: "We're all born Buddhas but I didn't see any at Mt, Hieu." A critical individualist, he traveled widely seeking enlightenment at many monasteries. He emphasized sitting meditation (*shikantaza*) to realize the "pure existence" of Buddha-mind and enlightenment and claimed that meditation actually *is* enlightenment. Soto values sitting meditation for its focused holistic effect and sees Rinzai koans more like focused mental exercises. Dogen considered master-student transmission over scripture study. Like **Tibetan Buddhism (Vajrayana),** Soto has a lineage bearer, usually a senior monk recognized as enlightened by a Zen master, appointed in a transmission ritual. Lineage is usually traced back to Buddha in a listed chain of transmissions.

Puhua (Chinese, **Fuke** in Japanese) was founded by Fuke, a Chinese student of Linji Yixuan who would walk through villages ringing a bell or playing the five-hole bamboo flute (*shakuhachi)* to awaken others to enlightenment. His music was "blown Zen" (*suizen*) to meditate. Shinchi Kakushin (1207-1298 CE), also known as Muhon Kakushin or Hotto Kokushi, spread Fuke to Japan after six years studying with Chinese Master Wumen. Most Fuke monks were not ordained. During the Edo period (1603-1867) *ronin* (rogue) Samurai joined and led to a reputation of Fuke monks as "troublemakers." Fuke weakened after the 1868 Meiji Restoration and was banned in 1871.

Huang-po (Chinese, **Obaku** in Japanese) was founded in 1654 CE by Chinese Yinyuan Longqi (Ingen Ryuki in Japanese) from Linji teachings of the 13th-16th centuries. It is "the most Chinese" but was influenced by **Pure Land Buddhism** that believed in salvation by faith and ritual to the Western paradise of ruled by Abidharma. Obaku monks were skilled calligraphers. Excerpts from Huang-Po:

As soon as you begin to reason you fall into error.

You are already fundamentally complete in every way. You already know all you need to know.

Buddhahood is not attained by stages or steps. There is nothing to be attained. That is the real Buddha.

There is One Mind, like the void where there is no evil or confusion, like the sun that is no less bright because it rises, sets, or is obscured by clouds.

The fundamental Dharma is eliminating conceptual thought and the craving and hate that accompany it.

DHYANA BUDDHISM FIRST PRINCIPLE

The basic first principle of **Dhyana Buddhism** is intuitive awareness of ultimate truth by *direct pointing.* Soto prefers sitting mediation (*zazen*) and Rinzai emphasizes **satori** flashes of insight and mystic leaps of consciousness. *Satori* can be a slow gentle nudge like an "I see" smile or the impact of an emotional "Ahah!" The mystic leap into the unknown has been called "falling off an imaginary log" or "going down the well." It is intuitive and inductive not rational or intellectual and often seems to defy logic. It is "caught not taught" realized directly and personally or by mind-to-mind master-student, not by traditional study or reading.

Language can be direct, sometimes crude or profane, to transcend the limits of words (*word drunkenness*) and empty the mind rather than adding more factual knowledge. In this sense you already know more than you need to know, probably too much. Your cup is overflowing. Empty it to enjoy a sip of Zen tea! The goal is mind "open as wide as the sky" and "as clear as a pane of glass," to see with a 3rd eye and hear with a 3rd ear. There is no mind, no knower, no known. What is, *is as is,* with no need to name, define, or change anything or anyone. It seeks the Buddha-mind inherent in everyone. There are references to inherent pure Buddha-mind in many texts. Here's a sample:

1. As the sun's light is never destroyed, only obscured by clouds or mist, the pure mind of everyone is hidden by clouds of superficial thinking, false   notions, and deluded views. Clear the mind of them and the Dharma sun of nirvana rises naturally. Thus, you realize the inherently pure mind-nature (Hongren, 600-674 CE).

2.   Go to the root. Do not chase after branches. At the root, everything will naturally follow. To find the root look into your own mind. It is the source of all, common and uncommon. When the mind arises, also dharmas arise. When mind wanes, dharmas wane. Allow the mind to rise above this and above good and evil, then everything is in its true state (Damei Fachang, 752-839 CE).

3. In your lump of flesh is a true person without rank always coming and going in the faces of everyone" (*Linji-lu*). This realization is *kensho*, the essence of Buddha's teaching, passed from generation to generation, like "water poured from one container to the next" (Linji Yixuan, ca 850 CE).

4.   Meditation is the substance of wisdom and wisdom is the function of meditation. When there is wisdom there is meditation. When there is meditation there is wisdom. Wisdom and meditation are similar. Meditation does not lead to wisdom, and wisdom does not lead to meditation, but they are not that different. This implies duality, like saying a mind can speak what is good but not be good. If mind and what is said are good they are the same   internally and externally. In this way meditation and wisdom are similar (Hui-neng, Teaching 13).

5. Thinking is not Zen. It does not lead to increased knowledge. Yet, you must think to realize Zen. It is not enlightening if knowledge is not increased. So, where are you now? How can you know Zen? When you fall into concepts and facts you're already a lifetime behind (adapted from Huai-T'ang).

6. A man was confronted with a tiger. He fled to a cliff and jumped off, but caught hold of a vine. The tiger snarled overhead. Below him was another tiger hungrily looking up at him. He held firmly on the vine, then saw two mice, a black one and a white one, nibbling away at the vine. There was a wild strawberry within reach. Holding on the vine with one hand, he reached out with the other and plucked the strawberry. How sweet it tasted!

7. Sayings of ChuangTse (Taoist):
   A scholar said to Mystic Unity: "I have seven openings by which I see, hear, breathe, and speak." Mystic Unity replied: "I do not have them." So, to provide them, every day the scholar dug a hole in Mystic Unity. After seven days Mystic Unity died.

   What is excessive is unnecessary. Start with too much wine and you finish word-drunk.

   Good fortune is lighter than a feather yet very difficult to carry. Chaos is heavier than the earth, yet it is very difficult to avoid.

   Enlightenment for the mighty wave begins when it realizes it is only water.

   I dreamt I was a butterfly. I was happy going where I wanted. I did not know I was ChuangTse. I was surprised when I awoke to find I was ChuangTse. Now I do not know if I dreamt I was a butterfly or a butterfly who dreamt I was ChuangTse.

8. Sayings of Master Chin Kung (Amida Society):

Where there is light there is shadow. Where there is length what is short becomes apparent. Where there is white there is awareness of what is black. So, nothing exists alone.

Life is an illusion, a dream, a shadow. Nothing is permanent and nothing is worthy of anger or conflict. Nothing!

Craving a passing pleasure is like a child licking honey from a sharp knife or holding up a torch in a strong wind.

When sitting quietly reflect on your faults. Look forward to those moments. Find your faults. Correct mistakes. Reform sincerely. Be kind. Concentrate. Rise above selfishness. Wake up!

When things go well, be mindful of misfortune. When prosperous, be mindful of poverty. When loved, be mindful of being unloved. When honored, be humble.

Saying pleasant words without meaning them is like a beautiful flower with no fragrance.

If you know anything hurtful or untrue do not say it. If you know anything helpful but not true do not say it. If you know anything hurtful but true do not say it. If you know anything helpful and true find the right time and say it.

When giving to others do not linger on the thought of giving, what is given, or the one to whom it is given. Just give.

Be mindful of the kindnesses and not the faults of others.

Receive kindness and never forget it. Be kind and never remember it.

Do not focus on the rudeness of others, what they do or leave undone. Focus instead on what you have done and left undone.

Forgive and be free. Forget you have forgiven and be even freer.

Until you have unbiased love for all beings you will not find peace.

Thousands of candles can be lit from a single candle and the life of that candle is not shortened. Happiness never lessens by being shared.

You already have perfect wisdom, perfect compassion, and perfect joy. You need only quiet your mind so they flow from within you.

As a slab of rock is unmoved by wind, the wise are unmoved by praise or blame. As a bucket fills by drops of water bit by bit, enlightenment fills you bit by bit.

Rely on a teacher's message, not a teacher's personality. Rely on meaning, not just words. Rely on real meaning, not the popular one. Rely on your pure mind-self and not your worldly biased mind.

9. Sayings from anonymous sources:
   Be here now. Don't push the river.
   Look lovingly at something.
   When you see a clear blue sky enter it.
   You can't step into the same river twice.
   The map is not the territory.
   What good would it do you if you had to go to the toilet
       and I went instead?

PARABLES
THE MISSING HEAD

There was a princess who was very upset because she could not see her own face because her eyes look out and not in. Her family assured her they saw it but she replied: "You just say it because you're my family." When a mirror was held up to her she said: "It's just a picture of me, not my head." In desperation, her father tied her to a post in the village square with a sign over her head asking all who passed by to reassure her she had a head. Many did, but it upset her more. She cried: "I can't see it. I can't feel it. I have no head." An old man walking with the help of a cane stopped and read the note. Suddenly, he swung his cane full circle and struck her on her head. She cried out in pain. "That," the old man said, "is your head."

SAMURAI SEEKING WISDOM

There was once a famous Samurai who was commander of the Emperor's Guard, a very high rank and status. It was time to retire and he wanted to learn philosophy, He went to a revered Zen Master who was rude to him: "Who are you and what do you want?" The Samurai identified himself and told of his wish for more wisdom. The master said: "I've never heard of you and you don't look anything like a Samurai. You look like an impostor, and a clumsy one at that." Irritated but still intent, the Samurai continued: "I'd like to learn about the meaning of life and about heaven and hell." The master said: "You are too stupid to learn anything." The Samurai, fire in his eyes, rattled his sword. The master persisted: "I see you have a sword. I doubt you know how to use it and it's probably too dull to cut anything anyway." Enraged, the Samurai drew his sword and raised it over the master's head, who then said calmly: "Now you have half the answer. The gates of hell are open to you." The Samurai, suddenly aware of his rage and its effect, dropped his sword and fell to his knees weeping. The old master put a hand on his shoulder and in the same calm voice said: "And now my son, you have the other half. The gates of heaven are open to you."

FORBIDDEN WOMAN

Two monks were begging food in the village, a daily task. It was the rainy season and streets were muddy. A very attractive woman in fine silk stood, afraid to cross the street. Without hesitation, one of the monks offered to help her. She consented and he picked her up and carried her across the muddy street. The second monk was very upset. All the way on the long walk back to the monastery he harangued his brother monk: "You know very well contact with women is strictly forbidden. We should never go anywhere near a woman, especially such a pretty one, all dressed in fine silk, and certainly never touch her." At the temple entrance, the first monk stopped and smiling graciously said: "My brother, I put that lady down hours ago but you are still carrying her"

THE GREATEST MISSION

Tetsugen was a Japanese Buddhist monk whose life work was to have Buddhist scriptures, then available only in Chinese, printed in Japanese. He traveled village to village to raise the money needed. It took him ten years, but at that time the Uji River flooded. There was a great famine and Tetsugen used the money to buy rice for the needy. A second time he traveled widely to raise the money. It took another ten years but then there was a great plague. He used the money to buy medicine for the sick. A third time he traveled to raise the money. It took another ten years and he was very tired but he lived to see Buddhist writings printed in Japanese. You can see them in the museums. But it is said by those who know they are not as good as his first and second editions.

FROM WESTERN WRITERS

The world is too much with us, late and soon. Getting and spending, we lay waste our powers and we see little in Nature that is ours. We've given our hearts away, a sordid boon (John Milton).

We shall not cease from exploring, and the end of all our exploring will be to arrive where we started, and know the place for the first time (T.S. Eliot).

The whole theory of the universe is directed unerringly to one person, namely, to you (Ralph Waldo Emerson).

There are more things in heaven and earth, Horatio, than are dreamt of in our philosophy (Shakespeare, *Hamlet*).

When I was coming down the stair I met a man who wasn't there. He wasn't there again today. I do wish he'd go away (Hughes Mearns, *Antigonish*, 1899)

KOANS (Japanese), KUNG-ANS (Chinese)

Koans or **kung-ans** are riddles to spark *satori* insight and enlightenment. They are not solved by factual knowledge. The student meditates on it, and then offers a solution to the master, usually a week later. If unacceptable, the student could be struck on the head with the master's a walking stick (*kyosaku*), often a fallen tree branch (reverence for life prevents cutting it from a living tree. Two examples of the thought processes involved:

1

STUDENT: What is perfect enlightenment like?
MASTER: Perfect enlightenment is like thieves breaking into
    a vacant house.

2

STUDENT: Is it useful to read the scriptures?
MASTER: There are no paths or crossroads but the mountain
    is always there, fresh and green, and regardless of the path
    you take, you can have a very nice walk.

Here are kung-ans/koans you can try. Remember, the object is a *satori flash* of intuitive awareness beyond logic and reason:

SIMPLE QUESTIONS
1. What time is it?
2. How well can you see?

3. When is your birthday?
4. How rich are you?
5. Who is your mother?
6. How old are you?
7. Who is your teacher?
8. What do you own?
9. Where is home?

BEST-MOST-WORST

10. Who is the best teacher?
11. What is the best knowledge?
12. Who is your best friend?
13. How can you know the most beautiful?
14. Who is your worst enemy?

COMPARISON AND PARADOX

15. What is the sound of silence?
16. How is failure success?
17. How is loneliness good?
18. How is leaving arriving?
19. How is ugly beautiful?
20. How is dark light?
21. What good is evil?
22. When are differences the same?
23. How can great be small?
24. How is empty full?
25. How is ending beginning?
26. When is man not a man and woman not a woman? When is a man a woman and a woman a man? And so?

KOANS WITH A LESSON

27. What is the lesson of emptiness?
28. What is a lesson of uncarved wood?

29. What is a lesson from a seed? From a flower?
30. What is a lesson from sunrise and sunset? Noon?
31. What is a lesson from water? The ocean? The beach?
32. What is a lesson from the wind? The sky? Clouds?
33. What is a lesson from a waterfall?
34. What is a lesson from snow? From ice? Rain? Dew?
35. What is a lesson from fire? From a candle?
36. What is a lesson from an insect? From a bird? From an animal?
37. What is a lesson from the earth? From the sun? From the moon?

CONTRADICTIONS?

38. How is a baby your grandparent? And so?
39. What effect would it have if a rose was called a weed? And so?
40. How is this a happy message: grandfather dies; father dies; son dies? And so?
41. Candle, wick, and flame, which is more important? How are they the same? And so?
42. Why give a lighted candle or lantern to a blind person? And so?
43. How can you reach higher on tiptoe from the highest mountain? And so?
44. Is there sound where there is no ear? Explain. And so?
45. How do you play the solid iron flute that has no holes? Explain. And so?
46. What is the sound of one hand clapping? And so?
47. Two persons argue. Both are right. Neither is right. One is wrong. Both are wrong. They teach each other but they fail the lesson. How can all this be? And so?
48. A boat sinks. Does water flow into it or does it lower itself into the water? Which is more powerful? Which

wins? And so?

49. How is black and white the same? How do they need each other? Which is more important? And so?

50. Hammer hits nail. Which is stronger? How are they similar? How are they different? Which yields more? Which wins?

51. There is a deadly snake and a piece of rope in a totally dark room with no windows or light. How can you know which is which? And so?

52. If you call this a sentence you are trapped by its name. If you don't, you contradict fact. What do you call it? And so?

53. Half of Zen is nonsense. Half of Zen is good sense. Half of Zen is both. Half of Zen is neither half. How can this be? And so?

54. Zen is nothing. Zen isn't nothing. Zen isn't know-thing. Zen knows. Zen no's. Zen nose. Zen knows nothing. Zen knows no-thing. Zen is something. Zen is anything. What is, is Zen, but Zen isn't it. Zen is, but isn't. How can all this be? And so?

THE RISE OF MAHAYANA BUDDHISM

What Buddha taught was passed down by word of mouth. It became **Theravada**, "the teachings of the elders" and also called **Hinayana**, the lesser vehicle or *Arhat* lone rider model of individual enlightenment. Buddha did not name a successor though there were many loyal followers to choose from, such as son Rahula or loyal cousin Ananda. As soon as three months after Buddha's death "Councils" were convened "to keep the Dharma pure." The first was at Rajagaha, attended by 500 monks. The 2nd Council at Vesali was held 100 years later and the 3rd Council at Pataliputta 200 years after that. The 4th Council was held in the Kashmir in the 1st century CE.

Despite the Councils there was branching and change as Buddhism spread to different countries, cultures, and languages. The earliest writings appeared during the 1st century CE, 500 years after Buddha's death, and in the language of the time and the receiving nation. Nagarjuna (160-250 CE), who some called "the 2nd Buddha," taught the **Middle Path** (*Madhyamaka*) between *u* absolute and *mu* nothingness, *sunyata emptiness* or *void*, the lack of essence and autonomous existence in everything yet interconnected, *tathata suchness* or as-isness, two levels of truth (ultimate and conventional or provisional), and a shared master-student transmission.

A major influence in Buddhist thought was the **White Lotus Sutra**, written written in the 1st century CE during the 4th Buddhist Council in Kashmir. It refers to "skillful means" (*upaka*) to impart truth and uses parables to do so. It describes the highest truth as beyond words. Buddha is hailed as eternal and having lived in other worlds. An excerpt: "All dharmas are the same, empty, and essentially without differences. Do not look to them to discern any separate dharma because the Dharma-body is one. There is no dyad or triad of vehicles, only one vehicle. To see this is to see Nirvana." *Sunyata* emptiness is seen as blissful, not entirely void.

In the sutra, Buddha's cousin Ananda quotes Buddha as saying: "The full truth is difficult to understand and can be unsettling, even incredible." He explains that Buddha's earlier teachings were suited to different levels of followers but there is only one way, the Great Way (Mahayana). Buddha tells the parable of the magic city and travelers to *The Place of Jewels*. A guide leads them through a dense forest. Tired, they ask to go back but the guide says they should go to a nearby town to rest. There, they eat and sleep. But there was no town. The guide created it by magic. He then leads them to *The Place of Jewels*.

Buddha explains that he is the guide, followers are travelers, and the *Place of Jewels* is Nirvana.

After more parables, Hinayana arhats become Mahayana bodhisattvas and Buddha asks everyone to preserve the *White Lotus Sutra* and hold it sacred. A stupa rises from the ground and a voice says: "Well done, Sakyamuni, you have taught the *White Lotus Sutra* and everything you said is true." It is Buddha Prabhutaratna of Abundant Treasure who lived millions of years ago. Sakyamuni generates a light ray and 500 Buddhas of the universe travel in it with their bodhisattvas. The Buddha Prabhutaratna asks Sakyamuni to sit with him. Sakyamuni levitates himself, all his followers and all the Buddhas and Bodhisattvas to join him and Buddha Prabhutaratna.

Sakyamuni says: "My death is near. To whom can I entrust this Sutra?" Everyone vows to preserve it, and he describes the traits bodhisattvas should develop: good conduct, undistracted focus on ultimate reality, a mind at peace, and loving kindness to all. He tells the parable of the Dharma Wheel King who rewarded his army with land, gold, and a precious jewel from his turban. He says he is like that king rewarding followers but with teachings of great value and the precious jewel is the *White Lotus Sutra*. He tells Buddhas and Bodhisattvas of the universe they are needed in their own worlds and calls them "my followers." He says his enlightenment was cosmic and not limited to one world and that he has lived in other worlds.

After another parable he emphasizes the karmic merit in the sutra, thanks all the Buddhas and bids them farewell saying: "Peace be with you. Let the stupa of Buddha Prabhutaratna of Abundant Treasures return as before." All rejoice and the great drama ends.

Pure Land Buddhism emerged in the 4th century CE from the teachings of Hui-Yuan (334-416 CE). Buddha was worshipped as Buddha Amithaba by devoutly reciting his name. Salvation is by faith to a Western paradise, the **Pure Land** ruled by Amithaba (not the heaven of western religions). Also in the 4th century CE, *Yogacara Chittamatra* "mind only" emerged in India based totally on subjective reality, and later spread to Tibet, Mongolia, China, and Japan. It is

Tendai Buddhism is the Japanese version of Chinese **T'ien t'ai** of Zhi-yi (ca 210 CE) and Chih-I (538-597 CE). It accepts all sects as aspects of the one Dharma and emphasizes the potential in everyone to become a Buddha. It claims the *Lotus Sutra* "contains all the Dharma," so *Tendai* has been called "the Lotus sect." Saicho (767-822 CE), brought it to Japan. He founded Mt. Hiei monastery which became a national center. *Tendai* was politicized by the Imperial family, nobility, and military leaders and stirred opposing popular sects by such ex-Tendai monks as Nichiren, Honen, Shinran, and Dogen.

written in the 1st century CE during the 4th Buddhist Council in Kashmir. We have no originals, only copies of copies. It refers to "skillful means" (*upaka*) to impart truth and uses parables to do so. It describes the highest truth as beyond words. Buddha is hailed as eternal and having lived in other worlds. An excerpt: "All dharmas are the same, empty, and essentially without differences. Do not look to them to discern any separate dharma because the Dharma-body is one. There is no dyad or triad of vehicles, only one vehicle. To see this is to see Nirvana." Emptiness (sunyata) is seen as blissful and not entirely void.

In the sutra, Buddha's cousin Ananda quotes Buddha as saying: "The full truth is difficult to understand and can be unsettling, even incredible." He explains that Buddha's earlier teachings were suited to different levels of followers but there is only one way, the Great Way (Mahayana). Buddha tells the parable of the magic city and travelers to *The Place of Jewels*. A guide led them through a dense forest. Tired, they asked to go back but the guide said they should go to a nearby town to rest. There, they eat and sleep. But there was no town. The guide created it by magic. He then led them to *The Place of Jewels*. Buddha explained that he is the guide, followers are travelers, and the *Place of Jewels* is Nirvana.

After more parables, Hinayana arhats become Mahayana bodhisattvas and Buddha asks everyone to preserve the *White Lotus Sutra* and hold it sacred. A stupa rises from the ground and a voice says: "Well done, Sakyamuni, you have taught the *White Lotus Sutra* and everything you said is true." It is Buddha Prabhutaratna of Abundant Treasure who lived millions of years ago. Sakyamuni generates a light ray and 500 Buddhas of the universe travel in it with their bodhisattvas. Buddha Prabhutaratna asks Sakyamuni to sit with him. Sakyamuni levitates himself, all his followers, and all the Buddhas and bodhisattvas to join him and Buddha Prabhutaratna.

Sakyamuni says: "My death is near. To whom can I entrust this Sutra?" Everyone vows to preserve it, and he describes the traits bodhisattvas should   develop: good conduct, undistracted focus on ultimate reality, a mind at peace, and loving kindness to all. He tells the parable of the Dharma Wheel King who rewarded his army with land, gold, and a precious jewel from his turban. He says he is like that king rewarding followers but with teachings of great value and the precious jewel is the *White Lotus Sutra*. He tells the Buddhas and Bodhisattvas of the universe they are needed in their own worlds and calls them "my followers." Asked to explain, he says his enlightenment was cosmic, not limited to one world, and he has taught in other worlds.

After another parable he emphasizes the karmic merit in the *White Lotus Sutra*, thanks all the Buddhas and bids them farewell saying: "Peace be with you. Let the stupa of Buddha

Prabhutaratna of Abundant Treasures return as before." All rejoice and the great drama ends.

Shingon Buddhism (Mantrayana) was founded by Kukai (774-835 CE), a Japanese monk who studied in China, then founded Mt. Koya monastery in Japan. His *Indications of the Three Teachings* described Buddhism as above Confucianism and Taoism by its focus on personal growth and character development. He called his movement *Shingon*, "the way of words" synthesizing body (*mudra*), speech (*mantra*), and mind (*master-student* interactiom). In 830 Emperor Junna ordered Buddhist sects to submit essentials of their belief. Kukai's formulation of *10 stages of consciousness* was chosen as best. It lists Kukai's evaluation of Buddhist sects, lowest to highest:

1. The Samsara self of worldly existence
2. The Confucian social self
3. Taoist or Brahman self
4. Hinayana awakening and partial understanding
5. Personal extinction by Hinayana nirvana
6. Mahayana opening of meditative awareness and in service to others
7. Nagarjuna's eight negations
8. Being 1-with anything in cosmic consciousness (Tendai)
9. Realizing the interdependence (Kegon)
10. Shingon Buddhism

Nichiren (1222-1282 CE) joined a Buddhist monastery when he was 16. He believed enlightenment can be attained by chanting the mantra *Nam-Myōhō-Renge-Kyō* and reciting the Lotus Sutra. Some Nichiren Buddhists meditate and chant to his *Gohonzon scroll* that includes that mantra. Nichiren was influenced by teachings of Saicho and Kukai but denounced Zen, Pure Land, Shingon, and other movements as deviating from true Buddhism. He was exiled twice and survived an attempted beheading.

These and many other movements departed from the **Theravada** lone rider model that was centered in monasteries and became **Mahayana Buddhism,** *the greater vehicle* (meaning shared like a carriage, not Theravada lone rider). It was aimed at saving everyone from karmic rebirths (the *Bodhisattva* ideal) and became the **2nd turning of the Dharma Wheel.** There are 14 classic Mahayana points of departure from Theravada:

1. Basis, origin is not limited to Sangha monks and nuns
2. Craving and clinging are to be overcome
3. The path should be shared and not traveled alone
4. Help others, do not escape the samsara alone
5. Mindfulness includes all phenomena and all dharmas
6. Mindfulness varies but is consistent with the *Six Perfections* (*paramita*)
7. Mindfulness is fitting for all beings
8. All dharmas are illusory
9. All dharmas are mind projections
10. Nirvana is beyond ending rebirths
11. Mahayana meditation is beyond ending rebirths
12. Mayayana attainment outshines others
13. Mahayana progresses through the *Ten Bhumi*
14. The measure of excellence is excellence

THE SIX PERFECTIONS (*paramita*)

To Mahayana, the Theravada model of seeking nirvana individually is a lesser attainment. Instead, it focuses on **the six perfections** (*paramita*) of charity (*dana*), meditation (*dhyana*), morality (*sila*), diligence (*virya*), forbearance (*kshanti*), and wisdom (*prajna*).

10 BODHISATTVA STAGES (*Bhumi*)

1. Joy (*paramudita*) rejoicing at realizing an aspect of truth
2. Purity (*vimala*), free of all defilements

3. Emit the light of radiating wisdom (*prabhakari*)
4. Glow (*archishmati*) with the flame of wisdom that burns away craving
5. Supreme wisdom (*abhimukhi*) slowly emerging
6. Overcome illusion and darkness (*sudurjaya*) by following the Middle Path
7. Progress (*duramgama*) rising above the two vehicles
8. Immobility (*achala*), unperturbed in the truth of the Middle Way
9. All-penetrating wisdom (*sadhumati*) in freely spreading the Dharma
10. Cloud of teaching (*dharmamegha*) helping all sentient beings as clouds rain impartially to all things

THE BODHISATTVA VOW
However many beings there are, I vow to save them.
However many defilements there are, I vow to extinguish them.
However many dharmas there are, I vow to realize them.
However incomparable enlightenment may be I vow to attain it.

MAHAYANA SUTRAS
From the DIAMOND SUTRA
3. Everyone can attain Nirvana.
4. True charity is always done in secret.
5. Material features are really non-material. Features are non-features.
10. Pure mind is no-mind. In reality, there is non-reality. Tathagata knowledge is formless, imageless, and transcending.
17. To value an ego-self or individuality is not a Bodhisattva quality. Nothing has an ego-self; it just is and is beyond better or worse.
21. Truth is indefinable.

25. Ego is illusion. So is non-ego. They are just words.
32. Fill worlds with riches and give it all away but to preserve, recite, and spread only a few lines of this sutra is far more valuable.

From the BLUE CLIFF RECORD

Interpretation of the highest. Emperor Wu asked Bodhidharma what was Buddha's supreme teaching, he replied: "It is Void of Void and more, where there is no distinction, not even of anything sacred or profane."

From the GATELESS GATE SUTRA

6. Buddha and the flower. Buddha picked up a flower. All were unmoved except Mahakasyapa who smiled, then Buddha said: "I hold in my hand the true Dharma, beyond life and death, form or formless, a great mystery that is beyond words and not transmitted by scriptures. I hand it to Mahakasyapa."

19. The ordinary mind of Tao. Jyoshu asked the Master Nansen: "What is Tao?" Nansen replied: "Tao is ordinary mind." Jyoshu asked: "Should we try to get it?" Nansen replied: "If you do, you miss it." Jyoshu asked: "But how will we know without trying?" Nansen replied: "Tao is beyond knowing and not-knowing. Knowing is false perception and not knowing is ignorance. Realizing Tao is realizing the whole universe. So, why argue about it?"

MAHAYANA SAYINGS

Wrong thinking leads to discriminating differences, such as subject and object, but there are none.

Appearances result from delusions inherent in our mental processes.

Numbers from one to infinity are self-sufficient but have no other distinct quality. Any distinction is one of convenience, only to indicate quantity.

The truly wise adjust to life with equanimity, neither puffed up by success nor shrunk by failure and in so doing they realize non-duality.

Words like good and evil, existence and non-existence, involve duality and lead to confusion and delusion. Be free of them to realize the sunyata void.

TO LEARN MORE
A good free search engine is: www.dogpile.com

DeBary, W.T. (1972). *The Buddhist tradition in India, China, and Japan.* New York: Vintage Books.

Humphreys, C. (Ed) (1961). *The Wisdom of Buddhism.* New York: Random House.

Hoffman, Y. (1975). *The sound of one hand: 281 Zen koans with answers.* New York: Basic Books.

Kapleau, P. (1967). *The three pillars of Zen.* Boston MA: Beacon Press.

Frank MacHovec (1972). *Tibetan book of the dead.* White Plains NY: Peter Pauper Press.

Frank MacHovec (2005). *Light from the East, a gathering of Asian wisdom.* Berkeley CA: Stone Bridge Press.

Frank MacHovec (2007): *Divine spark: Spiritual intelligence (SI) in you and the universe.* ww.lulu.com

Suzuki, D.T. (1956). *Zen Buddhism.* Garden City NY: Doubleday.

4
OTHER LIGHTS

TIBETAN BUDDHISM (Vajrayana)

Buddhism came to Tibet from northern India from both Theravada and Mahayana traditions, mixed with pre-Buddha **Bön folk religion** that honors Tonpa Shenrab Miwoche as its founder and not Sakyamuni Buddha. There have been several competing Buddhist movements in Tibet. The *Red Hats* are the Nyingma, Kagyu, and Sakya. The *Yellow Hats* or *Kadam-Geluk* represent "the new Tantric translation" in the Sarma tradition. Gelukpa (*way of virtue*) was founded in the 14th century by Je Tsongkhapa based on the Kadampa tradition and has a spiritual leader (Ganden Tripa) and temporal leader (Dalai Lama). The latter ruled Tibet from the 17th century to the 1950 Chinese invasion. There are also minor sects such as Jonang, Zhije, Bodong, and Buton. The Jonangpa were suppressed by the Gelukpa in the 1600s but survived in Eastern Tibet.

TANTRIC BUDDHISM (Tantrayama)

Tibetan Buddhism is also called **Vayjrayana** ("diamond vehicle or path"). It has three aspects: *ground, path,* and *fruit. Ground* is the practitioner, *path* is meditation to purify the ground, and *fruit* is the blissful, unified mental state. Tantric meditation transforms energy, develops concentration (*samadhi*), and expands consciousness. More than 1,000 years ago, Indian yogis of Bengal and Orissa began this movement as an esoteric (Tantric) aspect of Hinduism. In Sanskrit, **tantra** means "warp and woof that endure," non-dual oneness from interaction of opposites. It has been suggested that Buddha, born and raised Hindu, applied Tantric ideas of oneness and later Mahayana Buddhists adapted Tantric ideas to return to the inherent pure mind.

The classic Tantric Buddhist text "Union of Sun and Moon" reveals how to use right and left psychic energy channels (*nadis*) that radiate solar masculine and lunar feminine energies to realize wholeness. There are four kinds of esoteric texts which is why **Vajrayana Buddhism** is also known as **Tantrayana.** Tantra is sometimes misunderstood or misused in the West as eroticism. Most tantric practices do *not* involve sex though centuries ago sex was used to unify male and female solar-lunar spirits. In ancient India, it was *sacred sex,* such as *maithuna* using minimal movement, delaying orgasm to transform desire into spiritual consciousness, described as "melting, blazing fire into mystic heat" that frees the chakras (centers) selflessly and upward rather than in a narrow, downward, self-centered orgasm.

Today, some books and websites promote Tantra for better sex and even for financial success but it is more than that. Some tantric practices use diet, fasting, breathing and visualization meditation, chanting mantra, ritual mudra gesture, and subtle prajna energy channels, and kundalini yoga and body chakras to remove blockages and restore function. It is believed these practices strengthen the immune system and mental health. There is Tantric medicine in both the Indian *Ayurveda* and in the Tibetan Buddhist medical tantras where Buddha is *Bhaishajya-guru Buddha* teaching the *five medical tantra.* **Tantric yoga** is more intense than the **asana yoga** popular in the West and it is suggested it is best practiced with guidance from a tantric yogi or yogini.

TIBETAN BOOK OF THE DEAD

It is said Padmasambhava (c. 750 CE) hid the manuscript of the **Tibetan Book of the Dead** in rocks where it was found 600 years later. In 1919, American anthropologist Wallace Wendt rediscovered it in Tibet. The book describes the **Bardo Thodol,** "the journey of death," studied by the living to prepare for death, and read to the recently deceased to guide them to rebirth. There are three stages: *Chikhai Bardo, Chonyid Bardo,* and *Sidpa Bardo.* It can take up to 49 days to final judgment by the deity *Yama* who drops white or black pebbles for good and bad deeds. You can be lost for centuries, wandering before being reborn. Everyone searches for "the womb-door" of the next parent. **The guide** egins the book:: "With these teachings Buddhahood can be attained at the moment of death. If it is not, remember them and listen carefully when they are read to you. You can attain Buddhahood by hearing, remembering, meditating on, and being one with these teachings and what you experience after death … you will experience sights and sounds after death regardless of your religion and the extent you practiced it … even the most sinful can be liberated … if these teachings seem difficult, know that you can be liberated just by not disbelieving them."

KAKUAN'S BULL

Kuoan Shiyuan (Japanese: Kakuan Shien) was a 12th century Chinese Ch'an master who used taming a bull as a metaphor for enlightenment in a 10-step sequence, each step beginning with a statement seeking enlightenment followed by Kakuan's advice. It was believed enlightenment increased with each step.

1. THE BULL IS MISSING!

My path of life is like searching through tall grass for a bull.
I search unmapped territory and crossroads to distant
   mountains.
I tire. I can't find the bull.

Kakuan's advice: The bull was never lost! You are lost, separated from your true self and your transcendent nature. Your search fails because you are unaware of this. Your usual senses and skills do not help but weaken you and lead you to feel lost, alone, and the bull as missing. Without enlightenment it will get worse.

2. HERE – TRACKS!

Here, tracks on the river bank!
And there, more tracks through the grass!
They are as clear as the nose on my face.

Kakuan's advice: You do not see the bull, only outward signs that something was there. There is more to life than what you know. With greater awareness you will see the bull and not just signs left behind. You must choose: do you want to see what is there or what you want to see? That's how you got into trouble.

3. STOP -- BE ALERT!

Resting from the search I hear a bird singing.
The sun is warm, the wind mild, and the trees are green.
I still can't see the bull. It's not here.

Kakuan's advice: You will see and hear much more when you do not try so hard. The shade of trees is calming without your seeking calmness. Bird songs and soft breezes add to the calm. They seem to speak for themselves, stronger together than each alone, as if two and two are five. Use your own thoughts and senses like that. You will increase your awareness and see the way to the bull.

4. MAKE CONTACT, CATCH IT!

A gate opens. The bull! I wrestle with it.
Strong and stubborn, it runs away.
I feel high above the clouds or as if on a high cliff.

Kakuan's advice: You made contact but only for a short time. The bull goes where it wants according to its nature. It knows the territory better than you. You wander around according to your nature. The fact you made contact shows you are more aware now, but the bull's escape shows you need more skill.

5. TAME IT!

I found the bull and tamed it, but still it runs away.

If I can understand its nature I can tame it more.

Then it will stay with me and won't want to run away.

Kakuan's advice: Good. You are more open to what is and what is not. Let beings be. Simplify. A busy mind uses much time and energy. Overdo and you are so full what's important can't get in. Always start by letting everything be what it is by nature. Forcing anything is harmful to it and leads to evil and delusion. Open yourself and find your own true way.

6. RIDE IT!

I ride the bull and play the flute.

We keep time in harmony.

Is anyone listening? If so, come join us.

Kakuan's advice: As long as you, the bull, and anyone else, are open to their true natures there can be harmony. Feelings of failure or loss are then less relevant and less troubling. Realizing and doing this is to sing the song of birds, animals, fish, and children everywhere. Few hear it.

7. LET GO!

The bull and I arrive home.

We rest together quietly.

There is no need to do anything.

Kakuan's advice: Realizing there is one nature shared by all living things brings deep inner peace. There is no need to strain against any obstacle. Everything flows by its nature and all is well.

8. RISE ABOVE!

Differences fade sharing openly and truthfully.

The universe is vast, wonderful, and free.

It is enlightening to follow this path.

Kakuan's advice: There is no conflict and no stress when differences are seen as trivial and unimportant. Differences emerge of and by themselves, so there is no need to act for or against them or to form or reform them. This makes it difficult for anyone to know you since neither praise nor blame have any real meaning. Realizing no one owns anything or anyone brings harmony to relationships. Then perception is clear and limitless and the path upward is well lighted.

9. REALIZE THE SOURCE

It has taken a long time for me to awaken.

It's a lot easier to be blind and deaf.

To live naturally is like a blossoming flower.

Kakuan's advice: Truth and wisdom never change, beginning to end. It takes time to realize this. Enlightenment is silent. Do not seek it and you will find it. Ignore it and it is there. Mountains, valleys, oceans, and rivers are created and destroyed naturally, by their own natures.

10. TRANSCEND!

I interact as if naked before everyone and everything.

I am poor yet rich and happy and need no magic.

To me even the dead are alive.

Kakuan's advice: Realizing this step is like saying: "I am unknown. My garden is beautiful even if only to me. I do not need to search for enlightenment anywhere else. I work, walk outside, and return home, and everyone can feely share in this enlightenment."

MUSASHI'S FIVE RINGS

Shinmen Musashi or Miyamoto Musashi was a famous 16th century Japanese Samurai known as "the sword saint" (*kensei*), renowned for swordsmanship and wisdom. He won many duels. After fighting in the Ashigara-Ieyasu War where 70,000 were reported killed in three days, he Lived in a cave and spent his time meditating, painting, sculpting wood and crafting fine metalwork. In 1845 CE, just before he died at age 60 he wrote **The Book of Five Rings,** as much a meditative system as advice on war. Here are Musashi's five rings:

1st RING: Grounding-rooting

Carefully build the physical *way of the warrior*, the mental *way of the mind*, and a religious *way of morals* in a religion of your choice. Follow these nine rules:

1. Be honest
2. Train and master the way; maintain proficiency
3. Be familiar with all the arts
4. Be familiar with the ways of the professions
5. Know the difference between winning and losing, useful and useless
6 Develop intuition and higher awareness
7. See the unseen
8. Focus on details, the incidental and the important
9. Do nothing that is unnecessary

2nd RING: Be water

Be like water that takes the shape of any container. So, adjust to the realities of a situation. Water flows in a trickle or a torrent. So, apply yourself according to the need. Water is clear. Be as clear in your expectations and directions. Realize this and you know 10,000 things. Be steadfast, determined but calm. Meet situations openly, body ready but mind relaxed.

Do not let the enemy see into your mind. Be upright, head erect, brow unwrinkled, eyes open and alert, body balanced. This is combat posture. Perceive more than you see. See either side looking ahead. Use this in every situation, major or minor. Use weapons, tools, and material as if part of you. Develop *Yin-Yang* feet, equal, together. Be aware of the five aspects in every situation: left, right, above, below, and middle and realize that middle is the center and strongest.

3rd RING: Be living fire

Put yourself in the most advantageous position. Keep the enemy moving to lessen awareness of his position. There are three basic actions: attack, defend, or lock on. Attack is best but to win you must know the enemy's mind and strategy. Attack quickly but calmly. To defend, feign weakness and counter-attack forcefully when the enemy slows or shows confusion.

Lock on is to calmly continue a slow attack at weak points. *Holding down the pillow* is encouraging your enemy's useless actions then overcome them. *River crossing* is finding an enemy's weak point then carefully acting against it as you would cross a river. *Enjoining* is defeating one strong point after another like walking along a winding path. *Stepping on the sword* is totally defeating an enemy in body and mind. To prevent counter-attack, remain alert. *Penetration* is demoralizing the enemy as well as defeating him by war. *Crushing* is defeating the enemy so totally he has no resources left.

Becoming the enemy is thinking as your enemy thinks to better understand his plan and likely response. *Time testing* is closely observing what is happening then using the enemy's timetable against him. *Doing the unexpected* is using surprise effectively. *Passing it on* is to feign adjusting to enemy strategy then when he adjusts to it, suddenly changing and attacking. *Soaking in* is assuming the same strategy as the enemy to realize his weaknesses. *Fear tactic* is to upset the enemy with a small force that seems larger, or feign being more upset than you are. *Chaos* is keeping the enemy confused by constantly changing tactics. *Mountain and sea* is not using the same tactic twice. *Rat-head ox-neck* is changing quickly from one tactic to another and from minor to major detail. *Letting go* is decisive inaction. *Being* a *rock* is total commitment to the Way of Strategy.

4th RING: Change like the wind

Musashi saw the variety of beliefs and traditions as winds of change and recommended studying them "to see the Way in all of them. Winds blow from many directions, weak and strong, and often change. So it is with theories and beliefs, methods and materials. Being aware of this diversity but understanding their underlying principle is to see the Way. If you are not aware of this you are limited only to what you yourself know, a narrow path in only one direction. Most ways are not the *Way of Strategy* but the *Way of Strategy* is in all the ways. Some are narrow; some are wide. Some are strong; some are weak. Some overdo; some underdo. Some rely on quick awareness; some rely on deeper reflection or secret teachings. To win, use the enemy's weaknesses. To do that you must know all the ways of all enemies.

5th RING: Be no-thing

This is the Zen "mystic leap" of being so open you have no bias or fixed belief, mind open to whatever is, not what you want, fear, or need it to be. Musashi: "It is without beginning or end, open to the way and power of nature. Studying *the Way of Strategy* settles the mind and with daily practice 2-level thinking and feeling is refined into 2-level sensing and perceiving. Fixed belief, rigid systems, and believing all is well are not the Way."

FENG SHUI

Feng Shui (say "foong shwee") is an ancient Chinese system combining astrology, building orientation, and interior design for spiritual power. The goal is to maximize the flow of **Qi** (say "gee"), the life supporting universal force from **Yin-Yang** interaction of the five elements (earth, water, fire, wood, metal). **Feng** means wind and **Shui** is water -- wind-water force that joins the unseen mystic with material reality. As in Taoism, **Yin** symbolizes moon, earth, shade, and repose, drawn as two short dashes. **Yang** (dragon spirit) symbolizes sun, fire, light, heat, action and activity, drawn in one long dash. .

The five basic elements permeate the universe in mystic unity. The earth spirit was seen in anything flat, level, solid, and stable, in predictable situations. Water (rain) nourishes the earth and forests (wood), the source of wood for fire (cooking and comfort), and for refining ore (earth) into metal which melted flows like water, all in mystic interaction. Water force is in rounded or flowing objects and "fluid" situations. Fire is in pointed or erect objects and "inflamed" situations, wood in narrow or hard objects and "rigid" situations, metal in domed or shiny objects and "cold" situations.

Five pairs or 10 stems reflect the five elements: **Wu** and **Ji** as earth, rocky in mountains or sandy on beaches; **Jia** and **Yi,** hard and soft like wood; **Bing** and **Ding** as fire in lightning flashes and slow burning incense and charcoal; **Geng** and **Xin** as metal, finished or wrought from ore; **Ren** and **Gui** as water forms in rivers, lakes, ocean, rain, and snowflakes. These 10 stems are in the compass directions and also in birth signs: **Jia** and **Yi** are tiger and rabbit in the east; **Bing and Ding** are dog and ox at the center; **Geng** and **Xin** are rooster and monkey in the west; and **Ren** and **Gui** are pig and rat in the north.

The **swastika** is a Feng Shui symbol with no relationship to Hitler's Nazism. It was an ancient symbol in India, China, the

Middle East, Teutonic Europe, and pre-Columbian America. It was believed when it revolves clockwise it absorbed energy and when it rotated counter-clockwise it radiated energy.

The **magic square** or **river chart** is a table of numbers of uncertain origin. The most popular legend is a giant tortoise emerged from the Lo River about 2000 BCE with the magic square on its back. Another legend has it on a half-dragon half-horse that emerged from the Yalu River. Here it is:

N

8　1　6

W　3　5　7　**E**

4　9　2

S

Adding any line of numerals horizontally, vertically, or diagonally always totals 15. That was believed to make it magical and powerful. Numeral 5 is in the center, especially significant. Ancient saying: "The magic square stands on 9, 3 to the left, 7 to the right, and 1 is on its head." Numerals 2, 4, 6, and 8 are at the corners. This pattern was used to design palaces and temples for the number of rooms, hallways, stairs, and stories. Compass directions were seen as 9 south (highest and most favored), 1 north (least favored), 3 west, 7 east. Intermediate directions were 6 northeast, 8 northwest, 2 southeast, and 4 southwest.

Shapes and forms school. *Water Dragon,* the oldest Feng Shui manual, is attributed to Yang Yun Sung (ca. 600 CE). *Shapes and Forms* is based on *Chi, Qi, Yin,* and *Yang,* the four animals and five elements. The four animals: *green dragon*, *white tiger, tortoise,* and *phoenix.* Houses should face south with open entranceways (*phoenix*). The rear should face north with backdrop of shrubs, trees, higher land, or mountains (*tortoise*). East is *Yin* with a rising beyond by a higher building or wall (*green dragon).* West is *Yang* with rolling terrain beyond (*white tiger*). Streets or highways, entrances, doorways, odd- numbered steps and floors, and decorated walls are *dragon* symbols. Beds should be against a wall (*tortoise*), not adjacent
to a window (*tiger* or *dragon*).

Compass school. Wang K'e (ca 1000 CE) founded this school which added astrological and time perspectives from *8-house* and *Flying Star* theories on the Zodiac, 28 constellations, 64 *I Ching* hexagrams, *Yin, Yang, Qi,* and the five elements.

Principles school. Chu Hsi (ca 11th c CE) developed a system based on two factors: principle (*li*) reflecting the *Tai Chi Great Ultimate,* and matter (*ch'i*). Enlightenment depended on increasing *li* and decreasing *ch'i.*

I CHING
The Book of Changes

The **I Ching,** the **Book of Changes,** may be the world's oldest human relations manual. Evidence of its importance in ancient China is the saying: "With only the *I Ching* a corpse could lead the world." K'ung FuTse (Confucius) called it "the perfect book." That its advice makes sense today 5000 years after it was chanted, then written, proves its value.

According to legend, Emperor Fu Hsi (c. 2800 BC) was fascinated by markings on the back of a tortoise. On it he saw eight basic 3-line symbols: **Ch'ien,** *Yang* father, heaven, and creative force, as three solid lines; **K'un,** *Yin* mother, earth, and caring force, as three lines of two dashes; **Chen** first son force of action, movement, process, as two dashed lines and one solid line; **Sun** first daughter passive force of natural wood and calm air, as two solid and one dashed line; **K'an** second son flexibility and change, of sea and water, as one dashed line, a solid line; **Li** second daughter warming fire force of dependence and coexistence, as a solid line, dashed line, then solid line; **K'en** third son force of mountain stability, balance, and repose, as two solid lines and one dashed line; and **Tui** third daughter lake force of happiness and content-ment, as one dashed line and two solid lines.

FuHsi compiled 64 different hexagrams and believed they were the basis of life and behavior. He saw interaction in **Ch'ien** and **K'un** (heaven and earth), **K'en** and **K'an** (mountain and sea), **Chen** and **Sun** (storm and stillness), and **Tui** and **Li** (water and fire). It is also said that FuHsi developed writing, so the **I Ching** may be one of the first written books in China or anywhere else.

In ancient China, each hexagram or text was painted on a yarrow stick. Concentrating on a question or problem, the 64 sticks were held loosely in one hand, vertically, on a table top. The stick protruding most or that fell closest to the person with the question or problem was considered most relevant. A modern method is to use 64 slips of paper, each with a numeral from 1 to 64, folded three times, put in a container, shaken, then with eyes closed concentrating on a question or problem, one is selected. A variation is using 3x5" cards each numbered 1 to 64 and shuffled with eyes closed concentrating, then one card is randomly drawn or the shuffled cards placed face down and the top card drawn. Some find it helpful reading one hexagram a day for personal guidance.

The ancient Chinese also used the *I Ching* in small groups, like a town meeting. People faced north, then prostrated themselves three times. The formed a close circle, and sat with legs crossed (lotus position not necessary). The *I Ching* was passed clockwise through incense smoke, in silence, everyone concentrating on an agreed problem or question. When not in use the *I Ching* was wrapped in fine silk and stored as high in a room as possible, to preserve its purity and power.

SHINTO

Shinto has been called "the religion of Japan." There are about 80,000 shrines, small along roads and paths, in homes, to multi-acre sites. Shinto is involved in family, social, and political life, art, drama, and poetry, sports like Sumo wrestling, and spiritual life. Many events that are secular in the West include a Shinto ritual such as constructing buildings. Shinto has no founder, major scripture, creed or laws. There is no heaven or hereafter. It is ritual-based, so it is less a religion and more a part of the Japanese lifestyle. *Kami* are invisible spiritual beings and powers, not gods, who care about humans and are interested in them. Rituals communicate with them. Treated respectfully, *Kami* bring health, prosperity, and success.

FREE AUDIO DOWNLOADS
(from www.gutenberg.org)
The Art of War of Sun Tzu
The Travels of Marco Polo

GLOSSARY

Abhidharma. One of the tripitaka (baskets) of Buddhist Scripture.

Afflictions. See **defilements** and **klesha.**

Aggregrates (*skandhas, "heaps"*).Ways to perceive: (1) form sensed not thought, (2) sensed, pleasant or unpleasant, (3) named, classified, (4) mental processing, (5) final impression.

Akshobhya. Sambhogakaya Buddha. See **dhyani Buddhas**

Amitabha. Amida. One of five **Dhyani Buddhas,** the "Buddha of boundless light," depicted in red. Also the Bodhisattva who founded **Pure Land Buddhism.**

Analytical insight. 3-step process of contemplative meditation, 1-pointed concentration, and meditative awareness free of attachments.

Arhat, arahat, arahant (Theravada), lone rider model of individual attainment of nirvana.

Avalokiteshvara (Tibetan). God of compassion whose mantra is *Om mani padme hum.*

Awaken. Word often used for beginning to realize truth.

Ayatana. There are 18: six objects as seen, heard, smelled, tasted, touched, the six senses, and the six resulting consciousnesses.

Bardo (Tibetan "in between"). The state between death and rebirth. There are six in the *Tibetan Book of the Dead.*

Bhikkhu (male, **Bhikkuni** female). Ordained monks and nuns.

Bodhi, Bodhi-mind, Bodhicitta. Two kinds of enlightened minds: **absolute,** completely enlightened, and **relative,** committed to the six **paramita** and freeing sentient beings from **samsara** suffering.

Bodhisattva. An enlightened person who delays **nirvana** to help free all sentient beings from suffering.

Bon (Tibetan). The folk religion of Tibet before Buddhism and blended with it.

Buddha ("awakened one"). **Shakyamuni** or **Sakyamuni ,** the 4th and most recent **Buddha.**

Buddha-nature. The original pure mind-nature in all beings and when realized leads to Nirvana. Also called **essence of mind**.

Chakra (wheel or center). In **Kundalini Yoga**, a body center or channel where energy flows. See **dharma chakra.**

Ch'an, Ch'anna. Chinese for **Dhyana Buddhism.** In Japanese it is **Zen. Dhyana** in Sanskrit means contemplation.

Ch'i, Qi. "Vital breath," the basic life force.

Chittamatra ("to simplify"), the "mind only school, a major Mahayana school founded by Asanga (4th c CE) that only the mind is real and all phenomena are unreal.

Clarity, luminosity, clear light, a sign of empty mind. See **shunyata**.

Clinging. Attachment, from craving.

Consciousness. Eight kinds: five in **sensing** (seeing, hearing, smelling, tasting, touching), three are **mental** (processing, afflicted, grounded).

Craving. Currents of desire of lust, to be immortal, annihilated, in any of the six senses, their six objects, or in the mind. See **defilements**.

Dana. Unlimited, unconditional giving.

Defilements (klesha, hindrances), more emotional than intellectual. The three major **klesha:** passionate attachment, aggression and anger, ignorance and delusion. Five **klesha** are those plus pride and envy.

Definitive teaching is not adjusted to the hearer's level. **Provisional teaching** is adapted to the hearer's ability to understand.

Dependent origin is based on the 2nd and 3rd **Noble Truths** that suffering arises from previous thinking, not by chance.

Deva (god), **Devi** (goddess). Evolved beings still in the worldly **samsara** who need to attain **nirvana**. Hindu origin.

Dharma (doctrine, system, law). Capitalized **Dharma** is Buddha's unchanging teaching. Not capitalized, **dharma** is any truth. **Worldly dharma** are eight ways that block enlightenment: attaching to gain, pleasure, praise, or fame, aversion to loss, pain, blame, misconduct or bad reputation.

Dharani. Short sutra of mystic formulas or knowledge, usually longer than a mantra.

Dharma chakra ("wheel of dharma"). Buddha's original teachings are the 1st turning of the Dharma wheel (**Theravada**. The 2nd turning is **Mahayana Buddhism** and the 3rd turning is **Vajrayana Buddhism.**

Dharmadhatu. Essence of phenomena, the infinity of space without beginning from which all phenomena arise. **Tibetan Vajrayana** emphasizes emptiness of all phenomena.

Dharmakaya. See **kaya.**

Dharana ("holding steady"), early stage of meditation in conscious, focused attention on an object or idea.

Dhatu. Five elements in everything: **solidity** (earth), **fluidity** (water), **heat** (fire), **motion** (wind), and **function** (space).

Dhyana (Sanskrit "contemplation"), meditative concentration (**samadhi***)*, root word of **Dhyana Buddhism,** forerunner of **Ch'an** and **Zen**, and Buddha's final step on the 8-fold path.

Direct pointing, Linji Yixuan's method of direct personal enlightenment by **satori** flashes of insight.

Dorje (Tibetan), "diamond-like" **vajra**, a ritual object held in the right hand. Also a quality as pure as a diamond.

Egoless, egolessness, selflessness. Mahayana **Chittamatra School**, two aspects of egoless self and egoless empty existence, realizing a separate self is empty phenomenon and internal phenomena are without value, thus empty.

Ego-self. The selfish ego to overcome. See **mind-self, mind-nature.**

Elements. There are five, in matter and body function: earth, water, fire, wind, and space. See **dhatu, ayatana**

Emptiness (**shunyata** void). Mahayana concept based on Buddha's teaching that a selfish ego-self is undesirable, implying internal phenomena have no real existence and are void and empty.

Enlightenment. Lifetime goal of attaining **nirvana**, liberation from rebirths.

Essence of mind. The inherent pure mind-nature or Buddha-mind.

Eternalism, absolutism (*u*). Belief that anything is real or eternal.

Extremes, extreme beliefs in (1) the existence of everything (*u*, eternalism), (2) nothingness (*mu*, nihilism), (3) there is existence and non-existence, (4) brief reality as other than existence and non-existence.

Fearlessness. Bodhisattva stages of fearlessness: (1) abandon faults, (2) help others, (3) attain enlightenment, (3) point out obstacles to the path, (4) open to full realization.

Feng shui. Spatial arrangement of rooms and objects for the harmonious flow of *qi* energy.

Fetters, bonds. Five lower fetters are illusion, ill will, doubt, lust, and depending on rituals. Five higher fetters are: craving realms of form or formlessness, ignorance, pride, and restlessness.

Five Buddhas, Dhyana Buddhas (Tibetan). Aspects (traits) of Buddha in the five Dhyani Buddhas: Vairocana, Amithaba, Akshobhya, Ratnasambhava, and Amoghasiddhi.

Five precepts: Do not kill living beings; have loving kindness for them. Do not take what is not freely given; it is better to give than receive. Do not crave or cling; be content with what you have. Do not speak harmfully; speak kindly or be silent. Do not do anything in excess; be moderate.

Four Noble Truths. Buddha's classic original teaching about (1) suffering, (2) its cause, (3) its cessation, (4) the way of the 8-fold path to enlightenment.

Gautama Siddhartha, Sakyamuni, Shakyamuni. The 4th and most recent Buddha.

Gelug School. One of four Tibetan Buddhist schools, founded by Tsong Khapa (1357-1419 CE), now led by the 14th Dalai Lama.

Gradual School. The Northern School of Shen-hsui, the senior monk who unsuccessfully competed with "rice-pounder" Hui-neng to be 6th Patriarch. It disbanded after Shen-hsui's death. See **Sudden School** and **Rinzai Zen**.

Grasp. Initial understanding after **awakening**.

Ground, path, fruit. Buddhist way to explain a subject, by problem (**ground**), solution (**path**), and result (**fruit**).

Guru. Direct teacher. See **roshi**.

Hinayana (Pali "lesser vehicle"), the **Theravada** tradition of independent **Arhat** "lone-rider" search for enlightenment.

Hungry ghosts (Mahayana-Vajrayana). Spirit beings starving, thirsty, and needy, from excessive greed in prior lives, depicted with gigantic stomachs and narrow throats.

Immeasurables. The four aspects of enlightenment: unlimited loving kindness, compassion, joy, and equanimity.

Insight (vippassana) meditation. Develops insight into the nature of the mind. In **Theravada** it involves meticulously observing every thought. In **Mahayana** the emphasis is on the emptiness of all phenomena.

Jhana, Jnana. Enlightened wisdom beyond right and wrong.

Kalpa. Eon or cosmic age, usually millions of years.

Karma (Pali, Sanskrit **Kamma**). The law of cause and effect
or consequences. Your karma improves when doing
good and impaired when doing harm.

Kashyapa Buddha. Buddha who lived before the most recent
Shakyamuni or **Sakyamuni Buddha.**

Kaya. Mahayana conceptualization of three bodies of Buddha:
Nirmankaya human body, **Dharmakaya** truth body beyond
time and space, and **Sambhogakaya** bliss or **Bodhisattva**
body of mindfulness.

Kensha. Beginning and first insight into pure mind-nature.
An aspect of it is what you see also sees you.

Klesha (affliction, agony, poison). See **defilements.**

Kung-an, gongan, koan. In **Ch'an** and **Zen.** A riddle, dilemma,
or paradox to realize a flash of insight (**satori**) not solved or
explained by intellect or reasoning but by inductive intuition.

Loving kindness. Buddhist ideal from compassion for oneself
to compassion for others (**karuna**).

Luminosity (Tibetan **selwa**). Everything is void (**shunyata**)
but some clarity and awareness (luminosity) is needed to
realize it.

Madhyamaka middle path, a northern India Mahayana school
founded by Nagarjuna (2nd c CE) of a middle path between
u absolutism and *mu* nothingness, that all phenomena are
empty, though some reason is used to realize it (**upaya**).

Maha Devi. Buddha's mother who died seven days after he
was born.

Mahayana (great vehicle, the 2nd turning of the Dharma wheel
that emphasizes **shunyata** void/emptiness, service and
compassion (Bodhisattva), and to realize the inherent pure
Buddha-mind and Buddha-nature in everyone.

Maitreya. The next and 5th Buddha waiting in the pure realm
for the appropriate time to be born.

Mandala. A painting, print, tapestry, or sand tray of finely poured colored sands used to meditate, depicting a life landscape usually with a centered deity or sacred location.

Mantra. Spoken, chanted, or imagined word or phrase, usually in Sanskrit, of a sacred energy source. **Mantrayana** is **Vajrayana** Tibetan Buddhism.

Mara the destroyer. An evil deity said to tempt Buddha just before he atttained enlightenment. Also **defilements** of incorrect view of self (*skandha-mara),* overpowering negative emotions (*klesha-mara),* spiritual development interrupted by death (*mrityu-mara*), or stuck in the bliss of meditation (*deva putra-mara*).

Meditation (bhavana). There are two types: contemplative concentration (*samadhi),* and for serenity (*samatha*). The four foundations are: reflecting on precious human birth, the impermanence of life and inevitability of death, *karma* and its effects, and on *samsara* suffering.

Middle Way. Buddha's teachings based of the middle way between affluence and asceticism, often confused with the **Madhyamaka middle path.**

Mind-only mindfulness, Chittamatra School. The Mahayana Movement of Asanga (4th c CE) that mind is the only reality and everything else is illusion.

Mind-nature. Inherent pure mind, essence of mind, Buddha mind in everyone.

Moksha (Hindu). Liberation from karmic rebirth and craving.

Mudra. A "hand seal," hand or finger position or gesture that symbolizes a deeper meaning or state of mind.

Nirvana (Sanskit, Pali **nibbana)** "the extinguished," highest level of enlightenment free of delusion, craving, and clinging ending karmic rebirths.

Nihilism. See **mu.**

Nirmankaya. See **kaya.**

Noble Truths, Four: Life means suffering; craving is

suffering; it need not be so; the 8-fold path is the way to end suffering and rebirths.

Northern school. See **gradual school.**

Pali. Ancient Prakrit Indo-Aryan language (ca 1st c BCE) used by Theravadans in Sri Lanka, Myanmar, and Thailand.

Paramita (perfections). In Theravada there are 10: generosity, patience, resolve, moral conduct, renunciation, wisdom, diligence, loving kindness, serenity, and equanimity. Mahayana sutras list six: generosity, patience, moral conduct, diligence, wisdom, and 1-pointed concentration. The *Dasabhumika Sutra* adds three more: skillful means, knowledge, and spiritual power.

Parinirvana, parinibbana. Buddha's physical death not followed by rebirth.

Patriarch. Legendary leader traced back to Buddha.

Penetrate. Probing to realize hidden meaning.

Perfections. See **paramita**.

Prajna, panna: intuited transcendent wisdom. In Mahayana, realizing the true nature of anything as **shunyata emptiness** and **dependent origin.**

Prajnaparamita: Mahayana literature from the 2nd century CE on **shunyata emptiness**.

Prakriti form. Oldest sutra form, followed by Buddhist hybrid Pali Sanskrit, then Sanskrit.

Pratyeka Buddha (Theravada), a "self-realized Buddha" who attains **nirvana** without help from others.

Provisional teaching. Teachings fitted to the listener's level of understanding. See **definitive meaning.**

Qi, Ch'i. Vital breath, the basic life force. See **Feng Shui.**

Qi-gong, ch'i kung. Breathing exercises that free the flow of **qi** or **ch'i** force.

Ratna ("jewel"). The *three jewels* of Buddha, Dharma (teachings), and Sangha (fellowship, family of believers).

Ratnasambhava. The **Sambhogakaya Buddha**.

Realize. To "be one with" the real meaning of a teaching.

Realms. In **Tibetan Tantric Buddhism** there are six: gods; jealous gods; enlightened humans; animals; hungry ghosts; and hell of frenzied aggression. See **kaya**.

Rinpoche ("very precious"), term of respect for a Tibetan teacher.

Rinzai Zen. Japanese version of **Dhyana Buddhism** that evolved from Bodhidharma's "teaching beyond the Sutras," Linji Yixuan's forceful "direct pointing," and Hui-neng's "sudden enlightenment."

Roshi (mirror). One who *reflects* teachings but does not originate them.

Sakyamuni. Shakyamuni, Gautama Siddhartha, the 4th and most recent Buddha.

Samadhi. 1-pointed concentration, contemplation, meditative awareness. See **Sambhogakaya, kaya**.

Samsara. Worldly existence of everyday life and suffering, by a mind that is attached, craving, and delusional.

Sangha: "companions on the path," Buddhist monks, nuns, and more broadly, the family of fellows.

Satori. In **Dhyana, Ch'an, Zen** a sudden flash or gradually radiating insight. See **kung-an, koan**.

Selfless, egoless. A Buddhist ideal. In Theravada, the ego-self seen as a useless collection of thoughts, feelings, and images. In Mahayana, the ego-self has no inherent or real existence and is irrelevant to any other phenomena. See **shunyata, mu,** and **u**.

Sending-taking. Atisha technique when a meditator absorbs negative force from others, then replaces it with positive force.

Sensient beings. Humans, but A minority view includes animals, likely a Jainist influence.

Shakyamuni or Sakyamuni, Gautama Siddhartha, the latest and 4th Buddha.

Shamatha meditation. Meditation for tranquility by passively observing the workings of the mind to calm it. The 7th step of Buddha's Noble 8-fold Path (mindfulness).

Shariputra. One of Buddha's favorite followers known for reciting Sutras by beginning with: "Thus have I heard..."

Shastra. Writings or commentaries by anyone not a Buddha.

Shunyata ("voidness, emptiness"). Mahayanists believe Buddha taught phenomena and ego-self are not real but "empty" and devoid of meaning.

Siddhi. Special spiritual achievement.

Siddhartha Gautama, Sakyamuni, Shakyamuni, the 4th and most recent **Buddha**.

Sila. High moral conduct in behavior, speech, and occupation.

Skanda, skandha. See **Aggregates**.

Stupa. Usually a dome-shaped monument containing relics.

Suchness (tathagata). Things as they really are, as-is-ness, not as they appear.

Sudden School, of 6th Patriarch Hui-neng based on sudden enlightenment and direct pointing of Linji Yixuan that continued as **Rinzai Zen.**

Supramundane attainment. Three levels: **stream-enterer** (*sotapatti*), less than seven rebirths; **once-returner** (*sakadagami*), one remaining rebirth; **non-returner,** a final earthly life (*anagami*).

Sutra (Sanskrit, Pali **Sutta**). Teaching or "strand of thought."

Sutta Pitaka. One of the tripitaka (baskets) of Buddhst scripture, the one containing what Buddha said.

Tai Chi Chuan, Tai Chi ("ultimate way of life"), no-contact slow meditation to develop balance, flexibility, strength, for optimal health, formerly part of a martial art.

Tantra, Tantrayama (Tibetan). A **sutra path** studying **Mahayana** sutras. There are three kinds: **father,** to

transform aggression, **mother**, to transform passion,
and **non-dual,** to overcome ignorance.

Tathata (Sanskrit "suchness, thusness"), ultimate reality,
that everything and everyone are inter-related. **Suchness**
is the true nature of everything as is, in **sunyata** void or
emptiness, because **tathata is** "empty of predicates," not
definable, not just "empty." **Tathata** and **sunyata** "complete
each other." Theravada is skeptical of this concept.

Tathagata. "One who has come and gone before," Buddhas
and bodhisattvas.

Tathagatagarba: Buddha-nature, Buddha-essence in everyone.

Ten directions: the four cardinal directions, four interdirections,
up, and down.

Theravada: "Teachings of the elders," based on Buddha's
original unchanging teachings (**Dharma**), also called
Hinayana lesser or smaller vehicle, the Arhat lone
rider path to individual enlightenment.

Three immutables. Theravada, Mahayana, and Vajrayana
(Tibetan) Buddhism.

Three bodies. See **kaya.**

Three jewels of Buddhism (Ratna): Buddha, Dharma
(teachings), and Sangha (fellowship).

Tripitaka ("three baskets"): **Sutta Pitaka** (Buddha's teachings;
Abhidharma (commentaries); and **Vinaya** (monastic rules).

Truth. Two kinds: **relative,** of the unenlightened who see
the world by selfish projections and false beliefs; and
absolute, what really is and is not.

Turning the Dharma wheel. Theravada is the 1st turning,
Mahayana is the 2nd turning, and Vajrayana (Tibetan)
is the 3rd turning of the Dharma Wheel.

u. Extreme view of absolutism or eternalism. See **mu.**

Upaya. A means to an end, such as using reason to reach a
higher consciousness.

Vajra (Tibetan *dorje* "diamond like"). A ritual object held in
 the right hand; also, a quality as pure as a diamond.
Vajradhara. The **Dharmakaya Buddha.**
Vajra posture. The full-lotus position.
Vajrayana. Tibetan Buddhism mainly based on *tantras*.
Vijnana. Conscious thinking.
Vinaya. One of the triptaka (baskets) of Buddhist scripture, the
 one containing teachings on proper conduct, seven for
 lay people and more than 300 for monks, nuns.
Vipassana meditation, vipashyana ("looking in"), insight
 meditation on the nature of reality.
Void, emptiness. Mahayanists believe Buddha taught that
 all phenomena, external and internal, are projections
 of a selfish ego, have no real existence, and are therefore
 void, empty of meaning. See **suchness, sunyata, thusness.**
Yana. "Vehicle" or "way."
Yin-Yang. Mystic father (male) and mother (female) forces,
 manifested in the **Ch'i** or **Qi** life force.
Yoga (Hindu), literally to "yoke" to the universe by a system
 of posturing, movement, or exercise to enhance meditation,
 attributed to Patanjali in India.
Yogacara. Asanga's "mind only" **Chittamatra School.**

INDEX

OTHER BOOKS
by
Frank MacHovec

Light from the East. Berkeley CA: Stone Bridge Press, 2005.

From www.lulu.com:

Divine spark: Spiritual intelligence in you and the universe

Exploring inner space: The voyage of self-discovery

Pocket I Ching

Lead and manage: The four cornerstones.

www.ingramcontent.com/pod-product-compliance
Lightning Source LLC
LaVergne TN
LVHW011403080426
835511LV00005B/397